The Spirit of Robert F. Kennedy

Formerly titled *Bobby Kennedy Off-Guard*

compiled by
SUE G. HALL

GROSSET & DUNLAP

PUBLISHERS   NEW YORK

CONTENTS

INTRODUCTION

NO ONE WAS ever neutral about Senator Robert F. Kennedy during his lifetime. Perhaps it was because he never ducked a controversial issue. Whatever else he was or was not, no one could accuse him of being a fence straddler. Having read literally hundreds of his speeches to obtain the quotations for this book, I found that even when one might have disagreed with him, he was convincing — logical, concerned and eloquent.

The quotations were chosen to clarify, in his own words, the beliefs of Robert F. Kennedy. Now, after his tragic and untimely death, these expressions of his convictions stand as an eloquent memorial to his courageous life.

SUE G. HALL

ON POLITICS

I THINK WE can end the divisions in the United States. What I think is quite clear is that we can work together in the last analysis.

And that is what has been going on within the United States over a period of the last three years — the division, the violence, the disenchantment with our society, the division, whether it's between black and whites, between the poor and the more affluent, between age groups, or in the war on Vietnam — that we can start to work together.

We are a great country, an unselfish country and a compassionate country.

California primary victory speech
June 4, 1968, minutes before
his tragic assassination

PEOPLE ARE MAKING too much of my so-called conversion to liberalism. I was a liberal when I pardoned Junius Scales in 1962. But liberals had an

5

emotional thing about me, maybe because of Mc-
Carthy, maybe because of my Roman Catholicism,
maybe because of my fights with Humphrey and
Stevenson. I'm not that different now. I know more
now and I stay up late at night more often thinking
about these problems. But I was never all that
ruthless, as the liberals said.   *May, 1966*

PARTIES ARE INSTRUMENTS of government. They are
the vehicle by which the people achieve their aims.
What good are elections, if the party they elect
disintegrates when the time comes to fulfill cam-
paign promises? What does it matter to vote for
one man rather than another, one set of principles
over another—if struggles for personal advantages
and factional victory prevent those principles and
promises from being carried into effect? The business of parties is not just to win elections. It is to
govern. And a party cannot govern if it is disunited.
Speech, Kings County Democratic Dinner,
May 20, 1965

WHEN THE *Senator campaigned in New York to help
Justice Samuel J. Silverman win a primary against
the organization for Surrogate's Court, he talked to
children on the street.*

How many here have heard of Surrogate's Court?
Raise your hands.

A few hands go up.

How many of you study hard and obey your
parents?

More hands go up. Bobby grins.

Some in this neighborhood don't tell the truth, I'm afraid.

Laughter.

Now how many of you are going to go home tonight and tell your mothers and fathers to vote for Judge Silverman?

All hands go up.

Silverman, Silverman—you remember that name. Now let's go over it again. What are you going to tell your fathers and mothers when you get home?

"Vote!" the children answer.

And vote for whom?

"Kennedy!" they shout. Bobby puts both hands to his head in mock anguish.

To SAY THAT the future will be different from the present and past may be hopelessly self-evident. I must observe regretfully, however, that in politics it can be heresy. It can be denounced as radicalism or branded as subversion. There are people in every time and every land who want to stop history in its tracks. They fear the future, mistrust the present and invoke the security of a comfortable past which, in fact, never existed. It hardly seems necessary to point out in the United States, of all places, that change, although it involves risks, is the law of life.

Speech, 1964

I WOULD SAY that a genuine conservative or a genuine liberal sees that there may be more than one

way to resolve a particular issue. And he is willing
to engage in discussion and listen to the views of
others about what should be done.

*Television Interview in the WTTG Studios of the
Metromedia Television Network, May 15, 1966*

THEY ARE NOT going to vote for the Democratic
party because things are fine or because they "never
had it so good." They are not going the pull the
Democratic lever because they want to "stand pat"
or "keep cool." They will not favor our cause if they
want to keep the status quo or stand in the way of
change or go back to days that are gone. For if this
is the course they wish there is another party, the
Republican party, which is far better qualified, by
history tradition and temperament, to preside over
stagnation and drift. No, they will vote for us only
if they want to keep America moving. And I believe
they intend to keep America moving.

*Speech, Columbus, Ohio, October 8, 1966, Demo-
cratic State Committee Dinner*

WHEN MARSHALL McLUHAN told us that in this
century, "the medium is the message," he was doing
more than merely giving us a phrase to go with
"Keep the faith, baby." He was, in my judgment,
giving us an insight into modern politics, and a
disturbing one, at that. For more and more, as our
population increases, as the problems of our society
become more complex, and as the cost of political

campaigns continues to mount—it becomes more and more clear that the package is often more important than the product; that the perceived "image" of a candidate is often more important than what he says. That is one reason—I believe—why political parties are turning more and more to the prepackaged, pre-sold candidate. In the state that brought movie making to a high art, this has produced the new phenomenon of the actor as candidate—and a successful candidate at that. I think this is no accident. The cost of campaigning has become so high that to make a candidate and his views well enough known in a state like California or New York is impossible without either a well-known personality or enormous sums of money.

As an unknown virtually without funds, I was, of course, an exception.

Address, Skidmore College, February 22, 1967

I WOULD ENCOURAGE the many, rather than the few, to participate in public life at the national, state or local level.   *September, 1964*

THE CHALLENGE OF politics and public service is to discover what is interfering with justice and dignity for the individual here and now, and then to decide swiftly upon the appropriate remedies.

Speech, 1964

IT IS THE ESSENCE of responsibility to put the public good ahead of personal gain. This still leaves room for individual goals and for the pursuit of them with energy and intelligence. This of course applies to daily life—to the family—as it does to politics.

Speech, 1964

WE SHOULD NOT be disappointed that Community Action has not been an instant success. It has been a long time since most leadership in this country has spoken to the poor and tried to understand the problems of their existence. We should not be disillusioned because spokesmen for the poor have not appeared overnight. It takes time for genuine leadership capable of action and results to develop. Nor should we fear the conflicts that have arisen as new power groups contend with old, as political leaders are forced to meet the slum dwellers instead of the ward leaders. Every department of city government dealing with social welfare problems should feel challenged to justify their traditional response to the problems of the poor. They may not like it but the price of their discontent may be progress—and stronger and safer communities for our children and ourselves.

Address, Third Annual WGHQ Human Relations Award Dinner, Ellenville, New York, April 19, 1966

THE HOUSE, of course, is the sole judge of the qualifications of its members, as explicitly proved in the

Constitution. I am disturbed however, that the people of Congressman Powell's district are to be deprived of representation. I am also disturbed that this action was taken before the adoption of any uniform code of conduct applicable to all members of Congress, equally and fairly, extending not only to the use or misuse of government funds, but to every conflict of interest between the people and their representatives—for example, the acceptance of fees from groups interested in legislation; the practice of law with clients affected by Federal action; investment in companies regulated by or dealing with the government; and also the qualification of members elected in areas where qualified voters are denied their right to vote in defiance of the Constitution.   *Statement, January 10, 1967*

I BELIEVE THAT extremists of both the right and the left share certain characteristics. They are totally intolerant of the views of others and totally unwilling to engage in discussion. They don't have to because they have a simple answer for every problem.
Television Interview in the WTTG Studios of the Metromedia Television Network, May 15, 1966

THERE ARE overtones of violence to extremists movements, which I suppose is natural when one is unwilling to discuss his position.
Television Interview in the WTTG Studios of the Metromedia Television Network, May 15, 1966

THIS COUNTRY faces very complex difficulties internally—in the field of civil rights, in the field of poverty, in our relationship with communism, whether it be the Chinese or the Soviet Union kind —and great and complex problems in dealing with the undeveloped world. Some of our citizens feel that there are easy answers to these matters: The Communists are here and they've been here for 50 years. Why don't we threaten them with the atomic bomb? Why don't we make them disappear? . . . Let's get rid of Castro. Let's get rid of the Communists in Cuba. Why are the Communists in Berlin? Why do we have to put up with this behavior from 14 or 15 million people in North Vietnam? Why don't we just destroy them? The Negroes are causing unhappiness within our major cities. Why should they? Everything was fine five years ago. They were happy then; they were contented; and now they've been all stirred up. Why don't we go back to what it was like several decades ago? In the same way, there are those on the extreme left—those involved, for instance, in some of our civil-rights movements—who claim that if you're a white man you're automatically evil . . . These people have no confidence in the democratic will of the people, or our ability to develop answers to these problems over a period of time. They want these problems to disappear right now. They feel that they have to protect the Constitution, protect the white race, protect the womanhood of the United States and protect the country against Communism. So they turn to extremism.

Television Interview in the WTTG Studios of the Metromedia Television Network, May 15, 1966

As LONG AS we have difficult and complex problems, and as long as there are groups within the United States who feel that there are easy answers—that everything has to be seen in black and white, and that we can deal with these matters rapidly, without a great deal of thought and a great deal of time—we are going to have some extremism. As long as these same groups feel that they cannot have confidence in the judgment of democracy or in the American people, we are going to have extremism.

Television Interview in the WTTG Studios of the Metromedia Television Network, May 15, 1966

I THINK THAT we are also seeing a resurgence of extremism in the Northern communities. When we start to move in these areas, civil rights make some people uncomfortable, because things are not the same as they have always been.

Television Interview in the WTTG Studios of the Metromedia Television Network, May 15, 1966

THERE IS SOME indication that a third-party effort headed by extremist forces may occur in 1968. I think that if all of us—of all races and beliefs—act responsibly and reasonably concerning the internal problems now facing us as a nation, this extremist effort will not succeed. If we are firm against lawlessness and at the same time we remedy injustice fairly and expeditiously, then I believe that we as a people will be able to deal satisfactorily with the problems presented by an extremist political effort.

Television Interview in the WTTG Studios of the Metromedia Television Network, May 15, 1966

I THINK THAT the extremists of both the right and left can be identified by their inability or unwillingness to accept our system as the basic vehicle for social change, and their consequent lack of a program that we would call constructive.

Television Interview in the WTTG Studios of the Metromedia Television Network, May 15, 1966

I DON'T THINK it (the American Nazi Party) is a threat. I think they're a little like those people in the United States during that nostalgic period 30 years ago, who used to go around swallowing goldfish. I think we will always have people who are a little odd. And if you join the Nazi Party now you're very odd. I don't think it's a great threat and I don't think anybody pays very much attention to those people.

Television Interview in the WTTG Studios of the Metromedia Television Network, May 15, 1966

I DON'T BELIEVE the American Nazi Party is getting any great following. You always see the same five or the same six men. And so I'm not concerned with them as a great power, and I'm not concerned that they are going to receive any popular support. They're simply a bother and a nuisance and despicable.

Television Interview in the WTTG Studios of the Metromedia Television Network, May 15, 1966

THE JOHN BIRCH SOCIETY attracts a greater number of adherents because they say: "We could deal with Communism if it weren't for the kind of people who are now in Washington; China went Communist not because of her internal difficulties, but because we had traitors in the American Government. President Eisenhower is a Communist. That's why we have difficulty around the world. We can deal with Southeast Asia; we can deal with all these problems. Just follow us." That's an easy answer and something that people can identify with. You don't have to start thinking about it; you don't have to start working on it; and you don't have to try to come up with the complex solutions needed to deal with these problems.

Television Interview in the WTTG Studios of the Metromedia Television Network, May 15, 1966

I THINK THAT in some areas, over the period of the last few years, the Ku Klux Klan has gained in strength. Here again, the Klan offers easy answers to those who don't like the fact that the Negro in the South is beginning to come forward and express himself. The Negroes are beginning to vote. They might vote in some people who haven't commonly been accepted, or whose philosophy hasn't been commonly accepted. Join the Ku Klux Klan, the racist say, and you can end that.

Television Interview in the WTTG Studios of the Metromedia Television Network, May 15, 1966

BEFORE LEAVING *home one morning, the Senator carried the newspaper upstairs to his wife. When he came back downstairs, he turned to a friend and said:*

That's my good deed for the day. Now I can go back to being ruthless.

ON THE UNITED STATES'
ROLE IN THE WORLD

A LITTLE BOY [in a Russian elementary school], when asked to describe the United States, said, "The United States is a sad country where workers and peasants are starving under capitalist exploitation by the cynical ruling classes."

"Correct," said the teacher, "and what is the major goal of the Soviet Union?"

"To catch up with the United States."

Speech, New York, January 22 1963

NATIONS, like men, often march to the beat of different drummers, and the precise solutions of the United States can neither be dictated nor transplanted to others.

Address, Day of Affirmation, University of Cape-
town, June 6, 1966

FAR TOO OFTEN, for narrow, tactical reasons, this

country has associated itself with tyrannical and unpopular regimes that had no following and no future. Over the past twenty years we have paid dearly because of support given to colonial rulers, cruel dictators or ruling cliques void of social purpose. By achieving harmony with broadly based governments concerned with their own people, we do more than make our way easier for a year or two. We create for this country the opening to the future that is so essential.   *Speech, 1964*

EVER SINCE the onset of the cold war, we have been urged to "develop" a concise, exciting American manifesto—a platform which would compete with the simple, rousing calls of the Communists. Such an effort I think pointless—for what matters about this country cannot be put into simple slogans; it is a process, a way of doing things and dealing with people, a way of life. There are two major ways to communicate what this country is really about: to bring people here, or to send Americans abroad. *Address Sixth Annual West Side Community Conference, Columbia University, New York City, March 12, 1966*

IN MANY WAYS Wall Street is closer to London than it is to Harlem, a few miles uptown; Scarsdale is often closer to Paris than to Selma, Alabama; and Americans in Appalachia are in many ways closer to the Favelas of Rio de Janeiro than they are to the society in which you and I live.

Address, Testimonial Dinner for Congressman John Dow, Sterling Forest, New York, May 2, 1965

THERE IS, of course, freedom in the USSR to say the right thing. This was brought home to a young American visitor to Moscow who was earnestly explaining how any American could openly denounce the life and morality of the United States—even ridicule the President.

"It is the same here," said the guide. "A Soviet citizen may also denounce life and morality in the United States and ridicule your President."

Speech, New York City, January 22, 1963

I HAVE NO sympathy with those who are defeatists and who would rather be "Red than dead." Nor do I have sympathy with those who, in the name of fighting Communism, sow seeds of suspicion and distrust by making false or irresponsible charges, not only against their neighbors, but against courageous teachers and public officials and against the foundations of our government: Congress, the Supreme Court and even the Presidency itself. *Speech, 1964*

ULTIMATELY, Communism must be defeated by progressive political programs which wipe out the poverty, misery and discontent on which it thrives. For that reason, progressive political programs are the best way to erode the Communist presence in Latin American, to turn back the Communist thrust into Southeast Asia, and to insure the stability of the new African nations and preserve stability in the world.   *Speech, 1964*

WE CANNOT await with confidence the day when material wealth and a better understanding of economic reality will "bring China (or a new generation of Chinese leaders) to their senses." The history of our time gives ample proof that advanced, cultured and self-confident nations are fully capable of dark disorder, violence, and aggression . . . China may or may not become less aggressive and dangerous as it progresses—as the Soviet Union may, as Germany or Japan may, as we ourselves may. It is praiseworthy to hope and work for Chinese moderation; but to look upon moderation as the certain fruit of time, and act accordingly, is to tempt fatal danger.

WE KNOW that China is a difficult and hostile power and that negotiations with China may be frustrating —and perhaps fruitless. But China exists. China is a nuclear power. And without China's cooperation, the proliferation of nuclear weapons may be beyond our capacity to control. It is therefore our responsibility to take the first step—to take every honorable step— to bring China to the table of discussion at Geneva, or to engage in bilateral discussions at a high level elsewhere. But this we have not done. I think the Senate—I think the American people—are mature

enough and concerned enough about the problem of
nuclear weapons, to support such negotiations with
Communist China.   *Statement on May 17, 1966*

WHAT IS MORE troublesome is not what we do not
know about China; it is what we do not know about
ourselves—about our own goals, our own policies,
our own conception of our national interest in Asia.
. . . We have striven to isolate China from the world
and treated it with unremitting hostility. That, however, is not a policy. It is an attitude founded upon
fear and passion and wishful hopes.

THE POPULATION of this globe grows every day,
nowhere faster than in the underdeveloped nations.
In the next fifteen years, the population of Latin
America alone will be fifty percent greater than it
now is. Already, more than half the world's people
are under the age of 25; within a few years, the
majority will be under 18. We have it within our
power to give to millions of these young people a
greater chance at a decent life—to now have a major
effect on the course of their next thirty or forty
years. Millions are without schools—and we can help
to build schoolrooms; millions more are without text-
books, or teachers—and we can help to provide text-
books and train teachers; others cannot eat— and we
have food . . . A relatively modest investment now
can make a difference, in 5 or 10 years, to as much
as half the world's people—including our own.

Senate Speech, July 21, 1966

THE UNITED STATES owns more than half the total wealth of the non-communist world. The dozen developed countries of Europe and Japan share a total wealth about half as large as ours. The rest of the non-communist world—share a total annual production of something over $300 billion—less than half of what we, 6 percent of the world's population, consume each year. The developed nations as a group—twenty percent of the world's people—consume 80 percent of the world's goods. Fifteen years ago, rising to the challenge of a war-devastated Europe, we devoted ten percent of our Federal budget—fully two percent of our gross national product—to foreign aid. In 1960, under the Administration of President Eisenhower, we joined in the pledge of the United Nations' Development Decade—to devote a minimum of half that much, one percent of our gross national product, to the equally desperate needs of the newly developing nations. I believe the time has come to reaffirm that pledge, and to make it a reality.

Senate Speech, July 21, 1966

WE ARE ALL aware of, and delighted by, the success of the Peace Corps. The men and women who have served in it have brought to peoples around the world, in remote mountain villages and in bustling industrial cities, the true picture of the American of the sixties. It has been their spirit, their idealism, their skill and vitality which have done so much to erase the image of the "Ugly American."

Speech, 1964

WE ARE FINDING that it is not enough to feed and clothe and house a man—or even to give him work. Instead we are finding that the most important thing is to help men to help themselves. This is the most difficult task of all.

Statement before Students in Peru, November, 1965

WE HAD NOT been getting the truth about America to the world, particularly to the young intellectuals in the foreign nations, and particularly in those countries which are just growing, which have just come onto the world scene. Meanwhile, Communism, armed not with truth but with intensive, attractive propaganda, has been turning them against us.   *Speech, 1964*

OVER THE YEARS, an understanding of what America really stands for is going to count far more than missiles, aircraft carriers and supersonic bombers. The big changes of the future will result from this understanding or lack of it.   *Speech, 1964*

FOR OUR LEGACY—to our children, to the next generation of political leaders in the United States—will be far more than what we leave within our boundaries. Its most important element will be the role and standing of the United States in the world— whether, in short, people will look to this country with hope or with hate, emulation or envy.

Senate Speech, July 21, 1966

AN AMERICA piled high with gold, and clothed in impenetrable armor, yet living among desperate and poor nations in a chaotic world, could neither guarantee its own security nor pursue the dream of a civilization devoted to the fulfillment of man.

Address, Columbus Day Dinner, New York City,
October 11, 1966

EFFECTIVE AND REPRESENTATIVE government can, of course, take many forms. What is right for the United States may not be right for your countries, and others would have still other convictions on the precise form government should take—on ownership and control of the means of production, on the distribution of riches and the level of taxation, on the range of domestic and international policy. These questions must always be for each nation and people to decide for itself. So long as their choice is their own, not imposed from outside or by dictatorship of left or right, it must be respected by all others. If we wish to encourage the spread of democracy and freedom, primary reliance must be on the force of our example: on the qualities of the societies we build in our own countries—what we stand for at home and abroad.

Address, International Police Academy Commence-
ment, July 9, 1965

THERE MUST BE an unequivocal recognition, on the part of all countries in the Near East, that Israel is a nation, and that she exists. She has a permanent right to exist and grow and prosper. This is no longer open to doubt, and it can never again be open for question.

Statement on Arab-Israeli War, June, 1967

ISRAEL'S CREATION and her continuing progress in the face of continual adversity have written a new chapter in the annals of freedom and courage—a story that my children and yours will tell their descendants to the end of time.

Speech, American Friends of the Hebrew University,
New York, October 25, 1965

THE ALLIANCE FOR PROGRESS was not meant to be a means for the U.S. to determine the governments of every American nation.   *December, 1966*

THE DISPOSSESSED and the landless will not strive and sacrifice to improve land they do not own, in whose proceeds they do not share. Parents will not sacrifice to ensure education for their children, the children themselves will not study, if the schools to which they go end in the third grade. Individual entrepreneurs will not flourish in a closed society, a society which reserves all wealth and power and privilege for the same classes, the same families, which have held that wealth and power for the last 300 years . . . So a revolution is coming—a revolution which will be peaceful if we are wise enough; compassionate if we care enough; successful if we are fortunate enough—but a revolution which is coming whether we will it or not. We can affect its character; we cannot alter its inevitability . . . No matter how rich or powerful a nation may grow, children condemned to ignorance, families enslaved to land they cannot hope to own, are denied this dignity— the fulfillment of talent and hope—which is the purpose of economic progress. Progress without justice is false progress—and a false hope. Thus education and land reform must be at the heart of our concern for change in Latin America; and among the highest priorities of Latin American governments themselves. *Address, Eugenio Maria De Hostos "One-America" Award Dinner Society of Friends of Puerto Rico, New York, May 13, 1966*

WE ARE GOING to be held responsible for the failures and difficulties of Latin America. In many cases, this will be justified: we are further advanced; we are more fortunate; we do have a responsibility. But we are also going to be held accountable for far more than can fairly be laid at our door. This is a fact of life; it is important to understand that given the problems of Latin American educated classes, it can be no other way. So one consequence is that, if we are to judge our own actions fairly, Latin American criticisms of the United States should be placed in this proper perspective. *Address, Sixth Annual West Side Community Conference, Columbia University, New York City, March 12, 1966*

THE CONTRIBUTIONS made to this country by Spanish-derived culture through the ages are incalculable. Whether you are of Mexican, Spanish, Puerto-Rican or Latin American descent, you can well afford to take pride in the achievements of your ancestors. But taking pride in one's ancient heritage is always less fruitful—and less American—than taking stock of one's own recent past, his present, and his goals for the future. As Abraham Lincoln once said, "I don't know who my grandfather was, but I am much more concerned about what his grandson will be."

Address, American G.I. Forum, Chicago, Illinois,
August 23, 1963

THE RESPONSIBILITY of our time is nothing less than to lead a revolution—a revolution which will be peaceful if we are wise enough; human if we care enough; successful if we are fortunate enough—but a revolution which will come whether we will it or not. We can affect its character: we cannot alter its inevitability . . . America is, after all, the land of becoming—a continent which will be in ferment as long as it is America, a land which will never cease to change and grow. We are as we act. We are the children and the heirs of revolutions and we fulfill our destiny only as we advance the struggle which began in Santa Fe in 1580, which continued in Philadelphia in 1776 and Caracas in 1811—and which continues today.

Statement before Peruvian Students, 1965

OSCAR HANDLIN, the historian, observed: "Once I thought to write a history of immigrants in America. Then I discovered that immigrants were American history." Let us remember that history and look with confidence to the future, recognizing that our investment in new citizens will be repaid thousands of times over.   *Speech, 1964*

IT IS A SOURCE of anguish to many of our own citizens with relatives abroad . . . Under the law, an American citizen born in one country can get a maid or gardener overnight from another country but must wait a year or more to be reunited with his mother.
                                              Speech, 1965

THE FOLLOWING *exchange took place in Japan in February of 1962 between Robert Kennedy and Akira Iwai, a labor leader. Mr. Iwai's constant refrain was that the United States is imperialistic.*
KENNEDY: You call the United States imperialistic. Based on what happened in Tibet and Hungary, then do you consider the Soviet Union and China imperialistic?
IWAI: There were some mistakes made.
KENNEDY: Do you consider them imperialistic?
IWAI: We don't use that term.
KENNEDY: Why do you use it for the United States and not use it for them?
IWAI: Well, we determine it in the United States as monopoly capital.
KENNEDY: So I understand. It is permissible to

send troups in and kill people? Then one is not im-
perialist?

I mean, honestly, you know that the United States,
run by this Administration, is not made up of a lot
of monopolistic capitalists. Did you gather that from
Arthur Goldberg, who visited Japan some months
ago and who came from the Steelworkers Union? Or,
for instance, from me? Or from a country that raised
the minimum wage to a dollar and a quarter an
hour and passed all the other social legislation? Does
that make us imperialists? Capitalistic imperialists?

And the Soviet Union puts a wall up to keep their
people in this workers' paradise, and they march
into Hungary as they did, and you don't call them
imperialists?

As an amateur in diplomacy, it confuses me.

ON WAR AND PEACE

In November of 1967, Senator Kennedy held an informal talk with students in a Roman Catholic women's college. During his talk he took a poll on the Vietnam war by a show of hands. A large majority in the audience favored an increase in the bombing.

All of you who put your hands up, what are you doing to a lot of innocent people? Hundreds and thousands of people in Vietnam are being killed on our responsibility. You've got to think of the implications to your own conscience. . . . What makes us think they're going to give up? Would we go away if they started bombing us?

KILLING one man is murder; killing millions is a statistic. *Chicago, Illinois, June 21, 1961*

WITH THE IRONY of a paradoxical world, the surest

guarantee of peace at present is the power to wage war. The United States has that power. It comes from our programs of strength and deterrence. Without this strength we could not have achieved the truly momentous victory of the 1962 Cuban missile crisis. Without this strength we cannot reasonably expect to achieve other objectives even at the conference table in our constant pursuit of peace.

Speech, 1964

THINK JUST of the unparalleled opportunities for mischief: a bomb obliterates the capital city of a nation in Latin America, or Africa, or Asia—or even the Soviet Union, or the United States. How was it delivered—by plane? by missile? by car, or truck or ship? There is no evidence. From where did it come —a jealous neighbor? an internal dissident? a great power bent on stirring up trouble—or an anonymous madman? There is only speculation. And what can be the response—what but a reprisal grounded on suspicion, leading in ever-widening circles to the utter destruction of the world we know.

Senate Speech, June 23, 1965

GUNS AND BOMBS cannot build—cannot fill empty stomachs or educate children, cannot build homes or heal the sick. But these are the ends for which men establish and obey governments; they will give their allegiance only to governments which meet these needs.

Address, International Police Academy Commencement, July 9, 1965

I BELIEVE THAT, as long as the instruments of peace are available, war is madness. Governments must be strong wherever madness threatens the peace.

Speech, 1964

WE ARE STRONGER, and therefore have more responsibility, than any nation on earth; we should make the first effort, the greatest effort, and the last effort to control nuclear weapons. We can and must begin immediately.   *Senate Speech, June 23, 1965*

WE MUST ENSURE that those who threaten Israel know that she is not alone. We must continue to make certain that Israel is strong enough to deter any attack.

Address, Jewish Nazi Victims Organization of America, May 9, 1965

THE NEED TO halt the spread of nuclear weapons must be a central priority of American policy. Of all our major interests, this now deserves and demands the greatest effort.   *Senate Speech, June 23, 1965*

FULL AND INFORMING debate rests upon moderation and mutual indulgence. Men must seek acceptance of their views through reason, and not through intimidation; through argument, and not through accusation. We are all patriots here. We are all defenders of freedom. We are all Americans. To attack the motives of those who express concern about our present course—to challenge their very right to speak freely—is to strike at the foundations of the democratic process which our fellow citizens, even today, are dying in order to protect.

Statement on Vietnam, February 19, 1966

THE POOR MAN—the Negro, the Puerto Rican, the Spanish-American, the poor white—serves in Vietnam out of all proportion to his place in the population figures. And the casualty lists reflect disproportionate numbers of the poor as well. The Negroes and the poor in general bear the brunt of the fighting. We must intensify our efforts at home, for we must keep faith with the sacrifice they are making.

Address, Third Annual WGHQ Human Relations Award Dinner, Ellenville, New York, April 19, 1966

THE REAL POINT about sacrifice, except in times of open warfare, is surely that it tends to be undramatic, prolonged and irritating.

Address, Joint Defense Appeal of the American Jewish Committee and the Anti-Defamation League of B'nai B'rith, Chicago, Illinois, June 21, 1961

NO ONE LIKES Communism. No one wants Communism to win, or to dominate any nation. But the question is how we can best prevent the Communists from dominating South Vietnam—and, in the last analysis, what's best for the United States. What's best for the United States, in my judgment, is not an all-out war with Communist China, or a greatly expanded war throughout Indo-China. What we do want is not to let North Vietnam or the NLF take over. What we want is a settlement which stops the fighting, and saves American and South Vietnamese lives, and preserves the free choice of the people of South Vietnam. I think, if we continue our military effort, and pursue the social, economic, and political efforts which I've talked about repeatedly and which President Johnson emphasized at Honolulu, and pursue our diplomatic effort along the lines I suggest, we will at least know that we have done all that's now possible to obtain the kind of settlement we want. I think it is awfully important in our own country that we know what our objective is, so that we'll know what price in blood and anguish and money we're willing to pay to accomplish that objective. It's a different military objective to destroy the Communists within Vietnam. It's a different military objective to try to bring them to the negotiating table. And, from the recent statements that have been made, there is some confusion among various spokesmen for our own government as to exactly what our objectives are in Vietnam. But I do think we have brains, we have talent, and we have imagination in this country—and, if we can fight a war, then we can also work as diligently and as effectively to find a peaceful answer to it.

Press Release, Senate Office, March, 1966

WE HAVE A RESPONSIBILITY—to the rest of the world
and to our own children—to exert our best efforts of
thought and talent and energy to find a solution (to
the Vietnam problem)—not an easy solution, for
that does not exist; not a quick solution, for that does
not exist—but a solution which will preserve our
national interests without an even wider war in Asia.
Speech, New Hampshire Democratic State Conven-
tion, Manchester, N. H., September 24, 1966

WE MUST FACE the fact that what we need most is
a unified effort within South Vietnam. We must have
some certainty that the people of South Vietnam
can engage in such a united effort—that they have
the will and the ability to organize their society and
government to continue to fight. This is where we
should now be devoting our best efforts and talents.
We must face the fact that there is no quick or easy
answer to Vietnam. There is some disagreement with
our overall course in Vietnam. But even accepting
our basic policy, it appears to me neither prudent
nor wise to undertake risks of a still wider war until
some progress has been made toward achieving the
stability that is essential for the successful prosecution of our efforts in Vietnam.

Statement, Senate Floor, April 27, 1966

WE ARE CONCERNED about the effect of the war on
our domestic efforts to conquer ignorance and disease and unemployment—the problems of the cities

—problems which, warned the McCone Commission, could split our society irretrievably. And this concern is heightened by the way in which the war perpetuates discrimination—for the poor and the less fortunate serve in Vietnam out of all proportion to their numbers in the United States as a whole.

Statement on Vietnam, February 19, 1966

REGARDLESS OF one's opinion of the war, or of the bombings of North Vietnam, there is no justification and no excuse for the personal reprisals now threatened by Hanoi against individual American pilots. These men, in the oldest tradition of war, were following the orders of superior officers to attack targets which to the best of their knowledge were military involving no loss or damage to civilian life. They were doing their duty for their country—just as the soldiers of North Vietnam are acting according to their duty as defined by their leaders. I have dissented at many points from this war and its conduct. But I am at one with all Americans in regarding any reprisals among these young men and indirectly against their families, as an intolerable act—contrary to the laws of war, contrary to all past practices in this war, a plunge into barbarism which could serve the interest of no man and no nation.

Statement, Senate Floor, July 15, 1966

I BELIEVE there is a middle way, that an end to the fighting and a peaceful settlement can be achieved. It must be said, before all else, that the

middle way—the way of negotiation—involves risks.
An adversary who lives may perhaps fight another
day. And a government which is not continuously
sheltered by American military power may be again
attacked or subverted or overthrown. These risks, I
believe, we are courageous enough to undertake . . .
Whatever the exact status of the National Liberation
Front—puppet or partly independent—any negotiated settlement must accept the fact that there are
discontented elements in South Vietnam, Communist
and non-Communist, who desire to change the exist-
ing political and economic system of the country.
There are three things you can do with such groups:
kill or repress them, turn the country over to them,
or admit them to a share of power and responsibility.
The first two are now possible only through force of
arms. The last—to admit them to a share of power
and responsibility—is at the heart of the hope for a
negotiated settlement . . . It may come about through
a single conference or many meetings, or by a slow,
undramatic process of gradual accommodation.

Statement on Vietnam, February 19, 1966

IF WE ARE to leave our children a planet on which
to live safely, to fulfill the bright promise of their
lives, we must resume the journey toward peace.

Senate Speech, June 23, 1965

ON IDEALS

WHEN MR. KHRUSHCHEV reported that the Cosmo-
nauts—like the Bolshevik pilots of the early twenties
—reported seeing "no signs of God," we can only
suggest that they aim—with the rest of mankind—a
little higher.
Delivered at the 10th Anniversary Convocation,
Center for Study of Democratic Institutions of the
Fund for the Republic, New York City,
January 22, 1963

THIS COUNTRY has really been built on the founda-
tion that the government doesn't do everything; that
the neighbor helps his neighbor.   *Speech, 1962*

NO SOLDIER can tell us how to fight wars with
weapons that can destroy our world. No slogan tells
us how to educate poor people for competition in
the Twentieth Century. No political party platform

38

guarantees jobs for the victims of automation. No
District Attorney or Police Chief can offer a sure
way to cope with the increasing crime in our streets.
No political science text can tell us how to live in a
world where more than half the countries must live
on annual national income of less than the profits of
a single great American corporation. So new answers
must be found by us. They must be worked out not
only in the quiet contemplation of the study, but in
the dust and sweat, the swirl and thunder of the
arena. And they must be, above all, dispassionate—
determined not by the prejudices we bring to a problem, but by the facts we find in it.

Address, University of Alabama, March 18, 1966

MANY VOICES, many views all have combined into
an American consensus, and it has been a consensus
of good sense. "In the multitude of counselors, there
is safety," says the Bible, and so it is with American
democracy. Tolerance is an expression of trust in
that consensus and each new enlargement of tolerance is an enlargement of democracy.

*Speech, Dedication of the John F. Kennedy Inter-
faith Chapel, West Georgia College, Carrollton,
Georgia, May 26, 1964*

I THINK there is an obligation on the part of all of
us to stay informed and aware and to read the responsible newspapers and periodicals which discuss
national and international issues, and which themselves make an effort to distinguish between ex-

tremist exploitation of issues and legitimate debate and discussion.

Television Interview in the WTTG Studios of the Metromedia Television Network, May 15, 1966

THERE HAVE ALWAYS and everywhere been those, throughout our history, and particularly in times of crisis, who have preached intolerance, who have sought to escape reality and responsibility with a slogan or a scapegoat. Religious groups have been the first targets, but they have not been the only ones. There are those who suspect their neighbors because they pray to a different God, or because they pray to none at all. And there are those who bellow that a former President of the United States is a tool of the Communist conspiracy. There are those who preach that desegregation of the schools will destroy our society. And there are others who believe that calamity will occur because of the way we may treat our drinking water. There is freedom in this country to be extreme, to propose the most reactionary or the most utopian solutions to all the problems of the country or even the world. There is freedom here to believe and act with passion, whether for the cause of religion or party or personal welfare.   *Speech, 1964*

THE INTOLERANT MAN will not rely on persuasion, or on the worth of the idea. He would deny to others the very freedom of opinion or of dissent which he

so stridently demands for himself. He cannot trust
democracy.

Speech, Dedication of the John F. Kennedy Inter-
faith Chapel, West Georgia College, Carrollton,
Georgia, May 26, 1964

I BELIEVE THAT, as long as a single man may try,
any unjustifiable barrier against his efforts is a barrier against mankind. A government that can destroy
such a barrier without erecting any others in the
process is a good force. A government too weak for
that is not only a waste but an evil because it holds
out false hope.   *Speech, 1964*

THERE ARE THOSE, frustrated by a difficult future,
who grab out for the security of a nonexistent past.
Frustrated by change, they condemn the wisdom,
the motives and even the patriotism of those who
seek to contend with the realities of the future. They
search for the haven of doctrine.   *Speech, 1964*

THE FREE WAY of life proposes ends, but it does not
prescribe means. It assumes that people, and nations
will often think differently, have the full right to do
so, and that diversity is the source of progress. It
believes that men advance by discussion, by debate,
by trial and by error. It believes that the best ideas
come, not from edict and ideology, but from free
inquiry and free experiment; and it regards dissent,
not as treason to the state, but as the tested mechan-

ism of social progress. And it knows that diverse nations will find diverse roads to the general goal of political independence and economic growth. It regards the free individual as the source of creativity, and believes that it is the role of the state to serve him, and not his role to serve the state.

Speech, 1964

WHAT IS IT men want? Isn't it freedom of conscience and action conditioned only by the legitimate needs of private and public security?
Speech, 10th Anniversary Convocation Center for Study of Democratic Institutions of the Fund for the Republic, New York City, January 22, 1963

THE INDIVIDUAL MAN, in whose hands democracy must put its faith and its fate, is capable of great heights of achievement. He also is capable of infinite degradation. Fortunately most of our institutions have safe-guards which ultimately unseat a man when power results in arrogance and corruption. But often before justice is done the very institutions and values by which we attempt to order our lives can be undermined.

Speech, 1964

THP PEACE CORPS was and is the embodiment of the ideals that aroused our young people to a new level of commitment in the first place. It is premised upon the principle of humanitarian aid to nurture and protect individual dignity and security—a prin-

ciple that cuts across so much of what our young
people have done these past five years.

*Remarks, University of Southern California Convo-
cation, November 5, 1965*

IT IS FROM numberless diverse acts of courage and
belief that human history is shaped. Each time a
man stands up for an ideal, or acts to improve the
lot of others, or strikes out against injustice, he
sends forth a tiny ripple of hope, and crossing each
other from a million different centers of energy and
daring those ripples build a current which can
sweep down the mightiest walls of oppression and
resistance.

*Address, Day of Affirmation, University of Cape-
town, June 6, 1966*

IN THIS GENERATION we have seen an extraordinary
change in America—a new surge of idealism in our
life—a new and profound reality in our democratic
order. Much has been done. But much more must
be done, first because it is right, and because in
making equal opportunity a reality for all Americans, we make it a certainty for each American.

*Speech, Opening of Exhibit on the Emancipation
Proclamation at the National Archives, Washington,
D. C., January 4, 1963*

FEW MEN are willing to brave the disapproval of
their fellows, the censure of their colleagues, the
wrath of their society. Moral courage is a rarer

commodity than bravery in battle or great intelligence. Yet it is the one essential, vital quality for those who seek to change a world which yields most painfully to change . . . I believe that in this generation those with the courage to enter the moral conflict will find themselves with companions in every corner of the world.

Address, Day of Affirmation, University of Cape-
town, June 6, 1966

PROTEST FOR redress of just grievances is the right and the duty of every citizen in a free society. But protest must not be allowed to distract our attention from the job at hand—nor may the need of protest be used as an excuse for our own inaction.

Address, Borough President's Conference of Com-
munity Leaders, January 21, 1966

FREEDOM BY ITSELF is not enough. "Freedom is a good horse," said Matthew Arnold, "but a horse to ride somewhere." What counts is the use to which men put freedom; what counts is how liberty becomes the means of opportunity and growth and justice.   *Speech, 1964*

IN THE LIGHT of a truly freed mind no prejudice can disguise itself as zeal, no bullying can masquerade as leadership, no pettiness can pose as importance. The freed mind will never confuse a sentimentality with a true emotion, an act of violence

with an act of heroism, a slogan with a cause. Men
and women with freed minds may often be mis-
taken, but they are seldom fooled. They may be
influenced, but they can't be intimidated. They
may be perplexed, but they will never be lost.

Speech, Commencement Exercises, Trinity College,
Washington, D. C., June 2, 1963

IF OUR CONSTITUTION had followed the style of St.
Paul, the First Amendment might have concluded—
"But the greatest of these is speech." In the dark-
ness of tyranny, this is the key to the sunlight. If
it is granted, all doors open. If it is withheld, none.

Address, 10th Anniversary Convocation, Center for
Study of Democratic Institutions of the Fund for
the Republic, New York City, January 22, 1963

EVERY BUSINESSMAN who cheats on his taxes, fixes
prices or underpays his labor, every union official
who makes a collusive deal or misuses union funds,
damages the free enterprise system in the eyes of
the world and does a disservice to the millions of
honest Americans in all walks of life.

Speech, Law Day Exercises of the University of
Georgia Law School, May 6, 1961

CRITICISM IS characteristic of a committed population. But to be responsible and constructive, it must
be accompanied by continued participation, by care-

ful examination of the facts, and by consideration of the rights of others to speak.

Remarks, University of Southern California Convo-
cation, November 5, 1965

I FOR ONE would not be happy to see this nation bland and homogeneous, its speech and literature reduced to the common denominator of mass-circulation magazines, its life settled down into a uniform suburb stretching from coast to coast. What would *Abie's Irish Rose* have been if Abie was Jewish and Rose Irish in *name* only?

Address, Irish Institute, April 1, 1967

THE FUTURE DOES not belong to those who are content with today, apathetic toward common problems and their fellow man alike, timid and fearful in the face of new ideas and bold projects. Rather, it will belong to those who can blend passion, reason and courage in a personal commitment to the ideals and great enterprises of American society. It will belong to those who see that wisdom can only emerge from the clash of contending views, the passionate expression of deep and hostile beliefs. Plato said: "A life without criticism is not worth living."

Address, Berkeley Campus, University of California,
October 22, 1966

I BELIEVE THAT, as long as most men are honest, corruption is twice vicious. It hurts men and it undermines their fundamental rights. We must be doubly wary, with private and public vigilance.

Speech, 1964

IT IS NOT enough to allow dissent. We must demand it. For there is much to dissent from. We dissent from the fact that millions are trapped in poverty while the nation grows rich. We dissent from the conditions and hatreds which deny a full life to our fellow citizens because of the color of their skin. We dissent from the monstrous absurdity of a world where nations stand poised to destroy one another, and men must kill their fellow men. We dissent from the sight of most of mankind living in poverty, stricken by disease, threatened by hunger and doomed to an early death after a life of unremitting labor. We dissent from cities which blunt our senses and turn the ordinary acts of daily life into a painful struggle. We dissent from the wilful, heedless destruction of natural pleasure and beauty. We dissent from all those structures—of technology and of society itself—which strip from the individual the dignity and warmth of sharing in the common tasks of his community and his country.

Address, Berkeley Campus, University of California,
October 22, 1966

A CENTURY AGO Lincoln observed that the dogmas of the quiet past were inadequate to the stormy present. "As our case is new," he said, "so we must think anew and act anew. We must disenthrall ourselves."

Once again, our case is new; and nothing is more urgent than the obligation to disenthrall ourselves from the dogmas of the quiet past. Let us not suppose that we can freeze the United States—or the world—into the mold of today, or of a generation ago.   *Speech, 1964*

THE RIGHT TO criticize carries with it a responsibility —to study the facts, to be fully informed . . . So I would emphasize the debate and discussion must be based on facts, not merely rhetoric. And those who would criticize have a responsibility—to listen, to engage in a two-way discussion. Over and over throughout our history, both in this country and elsewhere, we have seen that it is the extremists who do not permit others to talk, who refuse to engage in discussion. It is the Communists and the radical right whose polemics will not stand up to the force of logic inherent in reasoned discussion. So if our young people—or anyone else for that matter—wish to criticize, I defend that. But they must also be willing to listen while others speak; and they must be willing to have their views tested in the marketplace of ideas.

Remarks, University of Southern California Convocation, November 5, 1965

ON THIS GENERATION of Americans falls the full burden of proving to the world that we really mean it when we say all men are created free and are equal before the law. All of us might wish at times that we lived in a more tranquil world, but we don't. And if our times are difficult and perplexing, so are they challenging and filled with opportunity.

Speech, Law Day Exercises of the University of Georgia Law School, May 6, 1961

JUSTICE IS LAND for those who live by farming— and all the world has seen that free farmers on their own land are the surest means to an abundant agriculture. Justice is a decent education for every child—and only with education for all is it possible to create a modern economy, to build and run the complex technology of the twentieth century. Justice is the absence of unearned privileges, and an equitable burden of taxes on rich and poor—and no nation can progress where the wealthy are taxed too lightly or the poor too heavily. Freedom is participation in the decisions of government—and only when the decisions are truly democratic, only when those who are affected take some part in their making, will they understand their meaning and join in their fulfillment. Freedom is opportunity to exercise one's talents to the full—unhampered by social origin, lack of wealth or the unreasonable dictates of others—and the society which limits that opportunity cheats itself of its most precious resources, the ability and energy of its people.

And in the end—in the simplest words, the greatest truth—must be recognition that in every man, in every child, is the potential for greatness—that all are the creatures of God and equal in his sight.

Freedom and justice—for me these are the meaning of America.

Statement before Peruvian Students, November, 1965

MOST OF OUR fellow citizens do their best—and do it the modest, unspectacular, decent, natural way which is the highest form of public service. But every day in a shameful variety of ways the selfish actions of the small minority sully the honor of our nation. The politician who takes bribes—the businessman who offers them—the industrialist who rigs bids and fixes prices—the trade unionist who works with gangsters—the God-fearing American who can't stand the idea of fellow citizens of a different color attending his churches or voting-booths—all have made a series of individual decisions which, one on top of another, degrade the whole character of our society.

Address, Joint Defense Appeal of the American Jewish Committee and the Anti-Defamation League of B'nai B'rith, Chicago, Illinois, June 21, 1961

ON DOMESTIC ISSUES

DURING SENATE *hearings in 1966 on auto safety, while Ralph Nader testified, Senator Kennedy engaged in the following dialogue with Senator Carl Curtis of Nebraska:*

KENNEDY: What I don't understand is why you don't let Mr. Nader read his statement to find out if in fact . . .

CURTIS: I have no objection to his reading his statement.

KENNEDY: Then maybe we would understand his position. . . . First, you admit you haven't read the book; and, secondly, you haven't heard his testimony. Why don't you listen to his testimony and then criticize?

CURTIS: I have no objection to hearing his testimony, but when he loses me with . . .

KENNEDY: With big words?

CRIME IS GOING to be a more serious problem in the

United States. Organized crime continues to spread its net into legitimate business and unions, corrupting politics and supporting local crime in every state and city. Many suburban parents, as well as those in city slums, must wonder at their children's irreverence for codes of decent and lawful behavior, as modern change assaults the deepest values of our civilization. And as more and more of our people crowd into cities, too often unemployed and unheard, living in slums and poorly schooled, there will be increasing frustration, increasing temptation to explode in violence. That violence is an intolerable threat to the future of every American—black or white—to the mind's peace and the body's safety and the community's order—to all that makes life worthwhile. We must prevent the repetition of violence—just as the underlying condition which gave it birth, the poverty and degradation of Negro life in the city, must also be a thing of the past.

Address at Dinner Honoring Congressman James C. Corman, Sportsmen's Lodge, Los Angeles, California, October 21, 1966

CARS CAN BE made more safe; but automobile manufacturers have not done so . . . All of us have learned from the advances in aerospace and aviation that we can have car brake systems that fail safe and not in a crash; that steering mechanisms can have a backup system that gives the driver control if the main system fails: that car seats and dashboards can be designed to protect rather than maim or kill . . . Americans know that we have the technical knowledge to build these devices—and that they do not need to be prohibitively expensive. Still the industry has claimed that the problems of brake failure, tire collapse and other major failures are beyond their engineering skill. These same manufacturers are willing to guarantee the reliability of complex missile and space systems they sell to the Armed Forces. The contrast is odd indeed. I submit that there is no lack of engineering ability in the United States today. The truth is that engineers are not asked to design for safety.

Speech to American Trial Lawyers Association, 1966

THE WAR ON poverty, like it or not, is the single outstanding commitment this nation has made to the principle that poverty must be abolished. Not just that fathers shall not be without jobs, and children without education, and mothers without medical care—though it is all of these. The war on poverty is a commitment to the principle that every American shall have the same opportunities to make a life for himself and for his own children—and the same opportunity to share in the government of his city and state and country, the same opportunity to share in the great enterprises of American public life.   *Senate Speech, October 3, 1966*

WELFARE WORKERS, or higher welfare payments, cannot confer self-respect or self-confidence in men without work—for in the United States, you are what you do.

Address, Borough President's Conference of Community Leaders, January 21, 1966

THE NURSING profession is losing too many of its members to marriage and motherhood and permanently. I am not against motherhood. However, of the 1,140,000 registered nurses in this country, only about 582,000 are actually working at the present time. For many of the rest, nursing is just not attractive enough to warrant the sacrifices and difficulties involved in raising a family and pursuing a profession at the same time. Now I am not going to discourage anyone from having lots of children. My point is that family responsibility and professional activity can be carried on side by side—if the continued professional activity is sufficiently attractive. And at present it is not.

Address, St. Peter's Nursing School, Alumnae Association, October 26, 1965

DELINQUENCY IS A broad problem and demands a broad attack. Educational programs, job opportunities, recreational facilities, adult counseling—all these projects and many more must be combined in a comprehensive program if we are to make a major impact on the problem. We must show every young person, no matter how deprived his background may be, that he has a genuine opportunity to fulfill himself and play a constructive role in American life. We cannot solve delinquency by building new prisons. We must create new opportunities for our nation's youth.   *November, 1962*

THERE IS SIMPLY not enough room in the big cities;

and it is not more bigness that should be our goal. We must attempt, rather, to bring people . . . back to the warmth of community, to the worth of individual effort and responsibility. Therefore, every step we take to make our rural areas more attractive and viable—participating in the economy, giving their children the finest possible education, affording their citizens the stimulus and excitement of thought and learning and entertainment—every such step is a gain for all America. For it was Athens, the very mother of cities, which showed us that greatness does not require size—even as others have shown us that size does not necessarily bring greatness.
Speech, Worthington, Minnesota, September 17, 1966

THE PLIGHT OF the cities—the physical decay and human despair that pervades them—is the great internal problem of the American nation, a challenge which must be met. The peculiar genius of America has been its ability, in the face of such challenges, to summon all our resources of mind and body, to focus these resources, and our attention and effort, in whatever amount is necessary to solve the deepest and most resistant problems. That is the commitment and the spirit required in our cities today.
Remarks, Model City Conference, Buffalo, New York, January 20, 1967

POVERTY LEADS TO crime, to lowered general prosperity, to higher municipal costs and a lower tax base; and where it causes early school dropouts, broken families, and the shattering loss of hope itself, poverty is self-perpetuating and self-generating. Education, the elimination of poverty, the building of a place of beauty and serenity—these are all things worth doing in and for themselves. But I stress their importance to business and industry because it is vital that all of us—those whose primary concern is business, those of us who work in government, and those of us who work in education, city planning, in agriculture, in recreation, in welfare—that all of us work together on what are really only parts of a single problem.

Address, Greater Utica Chamber of Commerce,
September 24, 1965

THE DATA COMING to light now shows that we have done all too little to rehabilitate and reintegrate into society those who have once run afoul of the law enforcement process. The rate of recidivism for released criminal offenders is far too high. The difficult question that now faces our nation is how best to deal with this recurrent cycle which continually brings those who have once had a taste of the criminal process back into contact with that process. From the little information that we have, the answer appears to lie in a greater commitment to rehabilitation. We must educate and vocationally train those who are in prison; and we must be prepared to supply guidance and help find employment for those who are released from incarceration facilities.   *Statement, Senate, May 17, 1967*

I VIEW THE businessman who engages in price-fixing conspiracies in the same light as I regard the racketeer who siphons off money from the public in crooked gambling or the union official who betrays his union members. A conspiracy to fix prices or rig bids is simply economic racketeering, and the person involved should be subject to as severe punishment as the courts deem appropriate. When possible, I believe that we should take action, not only against the corporations or companies involved, but against the individuals who have participated in these frauds. I am against granting immunity to the individuals, with the result that the responsible should be held responsible.   *Speech, 1964*

WHY SHOULDN'T YOUNG people who will be enticed to smoke by cigarette advertising be spoken for when the tobacco interests are heard so clearly? Why shouldn't the users of electricity be heard when the giant utilities are spoken for so effectively? Why shouldn't those who borrow from banks be heard as well as the financial institutions themselves? Why shouldn't the purchasers and viewers of the television sets be heard as well as the spokesmen for the networks and the manufacturers? Why shouldn't those who pay exorbitant prices for drugs be heard as well as the drug manufacturers? Why shouldn't the airline passengers be heard as well as the airlines? It is not easy to organize the consumers so that their point of view can be consistently and effectively set forth. But a Federal department, specifically charged with that obligation, could give the consumer the voice he needs, in the regulatory process.

Testimony, House Committee on Government Operations, U. S. Court House, Foley Square, New York City, April 29, 1966

WE HAVE A responsibility to the victims of crime and violence. It is a responsibility to think not only of our own convenience but of the tragedy of sudden death. It is a responsibility to put away childish things—to make the possession and use of firearms a matter undertaken only by serious people who will use them with the restraint and maturity that their dangerous nature deserves—and demands. For too long, we have dealt with these deadly weapons as if they were harmless toys. Yet their very presence, the ease of their acquisition, and the familiarity of their appearance have led to thousands of deaths each year—and to countless other crimes of violence as well . . . It is past time that we wipe this stain of violence from our land.

Congressional Record, Proceedings and Debates of the 89th Congress, First Session

THE FINANCIAL COST of organized crime is not limited to the vast illicit profits of gambling or narcotics. When racketeers bore their way into legitimate business, the cost is borne by the public. When the infiltration is into labor relations, the racketeers' cut is paid by higher wages and higher prices—in other words, by the public. When the racketeer bribes local officials and secures immunity from police action, the price exacted by corrupt law enforcement, incalculable in dollars, is paid, again, by the public.

Speech, 1964

IN TOO MANY major communities of our country, organized crime has become big business. It knows no state lines. It drains off millions of dollars of our national wealth, infecting legitimate business, labor unions and even sports. Tolerating organized crime promotes the cheap philosophy that everything is a racket. It promotes cynicism among adults. It contributes to the confusion of the young and to the increase of juvenile delinquency.

Speech, Law Day Exercises of the University of Georgia Law School, May 6, 1961

ORGANIZED CRIME IS a national problem. The racketeer is not someone dressed in a black shirt, white tie and diamond stickpin, whose activities affect only a remote underworld circle. He is more likely to be outfitted in a gray flannel suit, and his influence is more likely to be as far-reaching as that of an important industrialist. *Speech, 1964*

I BELIEVE WE must take a significantly greater action to discourage people from smoking at all and especially to discourage young people from starting to smoke.

Statement on Health Hazards of Cigarette Smoking, Senate May 17, 1967

ONE PHYSICIAN TOLD me recently that if he had his choice as a matter of health policy between immediately having enough doctors and nurses and hospital beds to remedy our serious national shortages in this areas, and getting every American who smokes cigarettes to stop, he would choose the latter. Far more lives, he told me, would be saved by getting the 48 million Americans who now smoke to stop than would be saved by solving all of our health, power and facility shortages.

Statement on Health Hazards of Cigarette Smoking,
Senate May 17, 1967

MY VIEWS ON birth control are somewhat distorted by the fact that I was the seventh of nine children.

After an effusive introduction:
I HAVE BEEN called a lot of things in my life, but this is the first time I have been called "beloved."

WE DEVELOP THE kind of citizens we deserve. If a large number of our children grow up into frustration and poverty, we must expect to pay the price.
Address to Young Israel of Pelham Parkway, New
York City, May 20, 1964

HAVE YOU EVER told a coal miner in West Virginia or Kentucky that what he needs is individual initia-

tive to go out and get a job where there isn't any?
August, 1964

OUR PUBLIC HOUSING efforts over the years, important and successful as they have been, have never
succeeded in erasing the plight of those entrapped
in slum housing. I would venture to say that one
reason for this—although I do not want to over-
simplify—is that the Federal Government has never
had a program for low-income housing which has
involved private enterprise in a meaningful way.
*Remarks, The New York State Home Builders Asso-
ciation, October 15, 1965*

AFTER A GENERATION of trying, it should be clear to
all that we simply do not have the legal and admini-
strative resources to chase every landlord in Harlem
through the courts and boards whenever the heat
fails or a window is broken. What is needed is to
put these buildings in the hands of people who do
want to keep them up.
*Address, Borough President's Conference of Com-
munity Leaders, January 21, 1966*

A COMMENT *to a friend:*
You're lucky. You've been poor.

I BELIEVE THAT, as long as there is plenty, poverty

is evil. Government belongs wherever evil needs an adversary and there are people in distress who cannot help themselves.   *Speech, 1964*

To RELY EXCLUSIVELY, even primarily, on government efforts is not only to ignore the shaping traditions of American life and politics, but to ignore the potential contribution of private enterprise is to fight the war on poverty with a single platoon, while great armies are left to stand aside. . . . Private enterprise has built our cities, and industries; it has created jobs for over 60 million Americans now at work. But it has not rebuilt the centers of poverty, nor put their people to work. And in my judgment, the lack of private enterprise participation is the principal cause for our failure to solve the problem of employment in urban poverty areas.

Remarks, Introducing Bill for Industrial Investment in Urban Poverty Areas; U. S. Senate, July 12, 1967

PROPERLY USED technology should not displace workers, but should speed them on their way to new jobs more quickly.

Senate Speech, June 28, 1966

SOME 75 PERCENT of those addicted to heroin come from the 20 percent of society with the lowest incomes. Until there are enough jobs to go around, until everyone has a decent home and a decent education, until we have uniformly stable and secure family structures—in short, until the world is a much better place than it is now—the mental problems associated with addiction—and addiction, itself, in one form or another—will continue to occur.

Statement, Union Baptist Church, New York, New York, December 6, 1965

SEVENTY-FIVE PERCENT of the drug addiction population comes from the 20 percent of society whose incomes are the lowest. It is hard to convince an addict that there really is hope, that he should seriously commit himself to a program which seeks to make him a member of a society that never before did anything good for him.

Senate Speech, June 9, 1965

SOCIAL SECURITY should be inflation-proof, and Congressional energy should not be expended on enacting benefit increases which do no more than make up for ground lost to rises in the cost of living.

Statement, Senate, February 16, 1967

MEDICARE FULFILLED a dream of a generation's standing, for social progress moves slowly and statutory reforms often lag behind scientific achievement and popular will. Its enactment took time, but it finally came, reflecting once again, as the Social Security Act did thirty years before, a recognition by twentieth century Americans that old age should be a golden span, an ever-lengthening period of health, happiness and productivity. But Medicare also imposes a great responsibility on us. It summons us to the task of ensuring not only that the cost of medical care is no longer a burden upon those who need but cannot afford it, but that good medical care itself is available. The bright hopes of Medicare can be dashed if we fail to achieve this, availability. What, after all, is the value of offering medical treatment to our aged if there are no doctors available to administer it? What is the value of offering nursing home care to our old people if there are no nursing homes where they can go? What is the value of offering hospital treatment to those aged who are seriously ill if there are no hospital beds waiting for them? The dream quickly becomes a nightmare; the bright promise becomes a dreary broken pledge; the loud trumpets announcing victory slide into a lower key of despair. Unless we as a nation are prepared, right now, to ensure that we have the facilities needed to implement the Medicare legislation, we would almost have been better off to have done nothing. If we are not prepared to move forward, energetically and imaginatively, to build on the blueprint of the Medicare legislation, then we had better be prepared for some very serious problems.

Address, American Medical Center, Judy Holliday Memorial Dinner, Waldorf Astoria Hotel, New York City, May 15, 1966

OLD AGE IS something that happens to everybody, and if we are wise enough and unselfish enough and

effective enough, then we can make those years a
time in which to live, not just linger.

Address, American Medical Center, Judy Holliday
Memorial Dinner, Waldorf Astoria Hotel, New York
City, May 15, 1966

OUR GREAT COMPANIES operate in every state in the
union. Their manufacturing operations are often
spread over dozens of states; they buy their mate-
rials and sell their products everywhere. The unions
which represent their employees are also national
in scope. For such a national economy to operate
efficiently and with a minimum of discord, it is
necessary that the laws affecting collective bargain-
ing and union organization not differ from state to
state. Lack of uniformity encourages states to compete with others for industry by making union organization more difficult. Even a Senator from New
York, which has lost large amounts of industry to
other states in recent years, cannot criticize the
efforts of less-developed states to attract industry
and the new payrolls it brings. But that competition
should not be fought out at the expense of American
workers, or of their rights to bargain freely on the
terms and conditions of employment—including the
union shop.

United States Senate, February 8, 1966

NO SECTOR OF the American economy, no group of
Americans, has made greater contributions to our
strength, our national prosperity, the health and

amenity of our lives, than the American farmer. In the last fifteen years, productivity has increased by 6.6 percent a year—more than twice as fast as productivity in the economy as a whole. They have provided the nation with the best diet in the world for a smaller part of our income than ever before, 18 percent today as against 25 percent in 1947— while people must spend 30 to 40 percent of their incomes on food in England, France and Italy, a full 50 percent in the Soviet Union, perhaps 80 percent in Africa, and 90 percent or more in many parts of Asia.

Address, National Farmers Union Convention, Oklahoma City, Oklahoma, March 13, 1967

UPON BEING INFORMED *that William Bufalino, president of the Detroit Teamsters Union, was suing him for $4 million damages:*

I think that Mr. Bufalino should take some of the union funds he's going to spend on this lawsuit and spend them for the benefit of some members of his local who are making as little as two dollars a day.

HOSPITAL ADMINISTRATORS striving to cut down spiralling costs are often guilty of treating nurses as second-class citizens. Doctors swamped with patients have delegated to nurses many of the duties they used to perform, an acceptable medical delegation, but an unacceptable numerical one because nurses are just not available for these extra duties. Hit from both sides, by both administrators and

doctors, the nurse suffers doubly. She cannot main-
tain the image of a perfect nurse who "must feel
like a girl; act like a lady; think like a man; and
work like a horse."

*Address, American Medical Center, Judy Holliday
Memorial Dinner, Waldorf Astoria Hotel, New York
City, May 15, 1966*

SCIENTISTS HAVE pointed out that 60% of the sea-
food taken from water surrounding the United
States is dependent on coastal bays and marshes for
their existence. If we destroy these wetlands, by
pollutions, dredging and landfill we will also destroy our fisheries. With 60% of our population in a
250 mile band along our coasts, the threat of destruction is not an ideal one. I need only point to
the complete loss of the oyster crop off the Connec-
ticut coast during the last year to indicate the
nature of the threat to our marine resources . . . A
shoreline with no fish, wildlife, or natural marsh-
land would be desolate. For these animals and fields
of march grass are as much a part of our heritage
as our mountains and great rivers.

*Statement on Long Island Wetlands Bill, before
House Subcommittee on Fisheries and Wildlife
Conservation, June 23, 1966*

ON A TRIP to Latin America last year, I saw people
in Recife, in the poorest part of Brazil, who ate
crabs which lived off the garbage that the people
themselves threw in the shallow water near their

shabby homes. And whenever I tell this story to Americans, the reaction is: how sad; how terrible; that such poverty, such underdevelopment, should exist in the world. But we New Yorkers are in a poor position from which to extend pity. For every year, the average New Yorker—old and young, rich and poor, athlete or infirm recluse—breathes in 750 pounds of his own wastes. The fuel which generates our electricity; the gasoline which runs our cars and taxicabs and busses; the four pounds of trash and garbage which each of us gives the city each day, and even the garbage we drop into our apartment-house incinerators—all these are discharged into the air we breathe. And because there are so many of us, crowding into this tiny fraction of the United States, a great pall of filthy air blankets the entire metropolitan area—and we all must breathe the same air into which we carelessly spill our refuse.

Statement, New York—New Jersey Metropolitan Air Pollution Control Conference, January 4, 1967

THE MILLIONS OF Southerners who were helped by TVA did not care that George Norris was a Nebraskan or that Franklin Roosevelt came from New York. And the millions of Northerners cured in Federally assisted hospitals do not care that Lister Hill is an Alabaman; the people of New York are not less helped by the Poverty Program because its enactment was secured by Phil Landrum of Georgia. And that must be the spirit of our future. For the problems of our day know no boundary of state or section.

Address, University of Alabama, March 18, 1966

I DO NOT BELIEVE that newspapermen are self-appointed judges of what's right or wrong, or what's good or bad. I believe in and greatly admire those who are competent to seek the truth and inform the people. In my opinion, the newspapers are equal to the courts—and sometimes ahead of the courts—in our system—in protecting the people's fundamental rights.

Address, Annual Luncheon of the Associated Press, New York City, April 23, 1962

YEARS AGO *in a conversation with a writer on his staff Robert Kennedy expressed his awe for someone who could make a living out of words.*

The only word the Kennedys know is "terrific."

Life Magazine, November 18, 1966

I THINK IT is very clear that a newspaper can be a major difference in whether an issue is going to be settled in the courts—or in the streets.

Speech, Conference of UPI Editors and Publishers, Washington, D. C., June 7, 1961

THOMAS JEFFERSON once said that he cared not who

made a country's laws, so long as he could write its newspapers. If this Congress goes on much longer, I'd rather be in the newspaper business, too. But the strength of the free press of this country goes beyond epigrams. The press is the base on which democracy rests in a complex twentieth-century society. I have worked in Washington for thirteen years, in the executive branch and in the Congress; and I know that the American press—vigorous and vital, critical and constructive—is essential to democratic government.

Speech, Western New York Publishers Association,
Painted Post, New York, October 9, 1965

ON CIVIL RIGHTS

THERE'S AN ACID joke about the Negro who attempted to register in a southern county. The registrar asked him to copy and interpret the 14th Amendment. He did so, brilliantly. "All right, if you're so smart," the registrar said, "recite the Gettysburg Address from memory." The Negro did. "Okay, give us the Second Inaugural speech." Again the Negro came through beautifully. Finally, the registrar pulled a Chinese newspaper out of his desk and asked, "Can you read this?" "That's easy," said the Negro, "It says, 'No Negroes are going to vote in this state this year.'"

Speech, Civil Rights Committee, New York City
Central Labour Council, AFL-CIO, New York City,
March 9, 1963

RELIANCE ON GOVERNMENT is dependence—and what the people of our ghettoes need is not greater dependence, but full independence; not the charity

and favor of their fellow citizens, but equal claims
of right and equal power to enforce those claims.
Address, NAACP Legal Defense Fund Banquet,
New York, May 18, 1966

WHEN WE SEE societies' failures—dropouts or dope
addicts, petty thieves or prostitutes—we do not know
whether they are Italian or English, Baptist or
Orthodox. But we know when they are Negro. So
every Negro who fails confirms the voice of prejudice.
Speech, National Council of Christians and Jews,
April 28, 1965

I MET THIS afternoon with members of the American
Society of Newspaper Editors in Washington and
we got along well, perhaps because some of them
realized I used to be a newspaperman myself. I
don't think I can lay claim to quite as close a bond
at this gathering. Nonetheless, I am pleased and
honored to join with you.
Speech, American Jewish Committee Appeal for
Human Relations, New York City, April 16, 1964

HOWEVER MUCH THE condition of most Negroes
must call forth compassion, the violence of a few
demand condemnation and action. In the streets of
many of our cities, in recent months, we have seen
riots and looting and even occasional murder. Still

far more disturbing than the chaotic, self-destructive violence of Watts or Oakland are the statements of a very few Negro spokesmen—those who have called for hatred to fight prejudice, racism to meet racism, violence to destroy oppression. Here is the seed of tragedy for black and white alike.

Address, Berkeley Campus, University of California, October 22, 1966

THE RIOTS WHICH have taken place—and the riots which we know may all too easily take place in the future—are therefore an intolerable threat to the most essential interests of every American, black or white, to the mind's peace and the body's safety and the community's order, to all that makes life worthwhile. None of us should look at this violence as anything but destructive of self, community and nation. But we should not delude ourselves. The riots are not crises which can be resolved as suddenly as they arose. They are a condition which has been with us for 100 years and will be with us for many years more. We can deal with the crises without dealing with the underlying condition—just as we can give novocaine to a man with a broken arm, without setting that arm in a splint; but the end result will only be more pain, pain beyond temporary relief, and permanent crippling of our urban society.

Remarks before Subcommittee on Executive Reorganization of the Committee on Government Operations of the United States Senate, December 10, 1966

EVERYWHERE WE LOOK, we find irrefutable evidence that the Negroes in America have yet to be given full citizenship, and we find increasing evidence, too, that they are no longer willing to tolerate the burdens we have imposed on them.

September, 1964

ULTIMATELY, WE MUST succeed in wiping out the huge central city ghettoes. By this I do not mean that the outcome will be racial balance in every urban and suburban neighborhood. Many Negroes, given a completely free choice, will choose to live in predominantly Negro neighborhoods just as members of other racial and nationality groups have chosen in the past to live predominantly among their own kinsmen. The important thing is that the Negro must have freedom of choice.

Address, Luncheon of the Federation of Jewish Philanthropies of New York, Americana Hotel, New York City, January 20, 1966

THE FIRST ELEMENT of individual liberty is the freedom of speech; the right to express and communicate ideas, to set oneself apart from the dumb beasts of field and forest; to recall governments to their duties and obligations; above all, the right to affirm one's membership and allegiance to the body politic —to society—to the men with whom we share our land, our heritage and our children's future. Hand in hand with freedom of speech goes the power to be heard—to share in the decisions of government which shape men's lives. Everything that makes man's life worthwhile—family, work, education, a place to rear one's children and a place to rest one's head—all this depends on decisions of government; all can be swept away by a government which does not heed the demands of its people. Therefore, the essential humanity of men can be protected and preserved only where government must answer— not just to the wealthy; not just to those of a particular religion, or a particular race; but to all its people. And even government by the consent of the governed, as in our own Constitution, must be limited in its power to act against its people; so that there may be no interference with the right to worship, or with the security of the home; no arbitrary imposition of pains or penalties by officials high or low; no restriction on the freedom of men to seek education or work or opportunity of any kind, so that each man may become all he is capable of becoming. These are the sacred rights of western society. These were the essential differences between us and Nazi Germany as they were between Athens and Persia.

Address, Day of Affirmation, University of Cape-
town, June 6, 1966

FOR AN AMERICAN man, woman, or child to be turned away from a public place for no reason other than the color of his skin is an intolerable insult, an insult that is in no way eased by the bland explanation that it has been allowed to go on for a hundred years or more. It is plainly a wrong and must be corrected.   *Speech, 1964*

WHEN OUR FOREBEARS—yours and mine—came to America, they came because this country promised them something. It promised them an opportunity, nourished by education, not merely to grind for a bare living, but to strive for a good life.
Speech, Young Israel of Pelham Parkway, New York City, May 20, 1964

IT IS THE ideal of freedom which underlies our great concern for civil rights. Nations around the world look to us for leadership not merely by strength of arms but by the strength of our convictions. We not only want, but we need, the free exercise of rights by every American. We need the strength and talent of every American. We need, in short, to set an example of freedom for the world—and for ourselves.
Address, American Jewish Congress, New York City, October 28, 1962

LIKE OTHER MINORITY groups, Negroes will bear the major burden of their own progress. They will have to make their own way, as they are doing. But we must remember that other minorities, including my own, also make progress through increasing their political and economic power as well as by individual effort. Nor was that progress completely without violence, fear and hatred. Moreover earlier immigrants often began their cities by moving to the unsettled West, a door now closed; or finding unskilled labor, a door which is swiftly narrowing. Today to find a job requires increasingly complex skills, denied to those without education. Nor did other minorities suffer under the special handicaps of the Negro heritage—centuries of slavery and a century of oppression, an intricate web of legal disabilities, and the crushing forces of racial feeling from whose poisons few whites have fully liberated themselves.

Address, Berkeley Campus, University of California,
October 22, 1966

FROM TIME *to time during Robert Kennedy's term as Attorney General, he found himself the object of civil rights demonstrations. On one occasion he encountered a group of Negroes parading before the Justice Department building, protesting discrimination in employment, and declared:*
Any individual can come in here and get a job if he is qualified. . . . But I'm not going out and hire a Negro just because he's not white.

June 14, 1963

YOU MAY ASK, will we enforce the civil rights statutes? The answer is, "Yes, we will." We will also enforce the antitrust laws, the antiracketeering laws, the laws against kidnaping and robbing Federal banks and transporting stolen automobiles across state lines, the illicit traffic in narcotics and all the rest . . . I hold a constitutional office of the United States Government, and I shall perform the duty I have sworn to undertake: to enforce the law, in every field of law, without regional bias or political slant.

Law Day Address, University of Georgia Law School, Athens, Georgia, May 5, 1961

THOSE OF US who are white can only dimly guess at what the pain of racial discrimination must be— what it must be like to be turned away from a public place, or made to use only a segregated portion of that place, for no reason other than the color of one's skin. Prostitutes, criminals, Communist and Fascist conspirators—these people are free to go to the movies and to choose their own seats, as long as they are white. How can a Negro father explain this intolerable situation to his children? And how can the children be expected to grow up with any sense of pride in being Americans?

Address, Annual Convention of the Theater Owners of America, New York City, October 28, 1963

SOME FINANCIAL LEADERS from the East who deplore discrimination in the South belong to institutions where no Negroes or Jews are allowed and their children often attend private schools where no Negro students are enrolled. Union officials criticize Southern leaders and yet practice discrimination

within their unions. Government officials belong to
private clubs in Washington where Negroes, including Ambassadors, are not welcome—even at meal-
time.

Speech, Law Day Exercises of the University of
Georgia Law School, May 6, 1961

IT IS IMPORTANT that Negroes who have achieved
financial and social security should have complete
freedom to choose where to live. But it is far more
important that the vast majority of Negroes be
enabled to achieve basic financial and social security
where they live now.

Remarks before Subcommittee on Executive Reorgan-
ization of the Committee on Government Operations
of the United States Senate, December 10, 1966

MILITARY AND POLICE law have been needed to
replace normal local rule in countless cities in the
North as well as the South. This is what happens
when long-standing legitimate grievances are not
remedied under law. Great moral damage is done
to individuals, to communities, to states and to the
very fabric of the nation. We cannot excuse violence
from any source or from any group. The responsibility of the Negro leaders who set these demonstrations in motion is very great, as is the responsibility
of the white leadership in every community. But
our responsibility as a nation is most plain. We must
remove the injustices.   *Speech, 1964*

THE CRISIS IN Negro unemployment is significant far beyond its economic effects—devastating as those are. For it is both measure and cause of the extent to which the Negro lives apart—the extent to which he is alienated from the general community. More than segregation in housing and schools, more than differences in attitudes or life-style, it is unemployment which marks the Negro of the urban ghetto off and apart from the rest of us—from Negroes who have jobs (including Negro leaders) almost as much as from whites. Unemployment is having nothing to do—which means having nothing to do with the rest of us.

Remarks before Subcommittee on Executive Reorganization of the Committee on Government Operations of the United States Senate, December 10, 1966

THE ARMY OF the resentful and desperate in the North is an army without generals . . . without captains . . . almost without sergeants. . . . Too many Negroes who have succeeded in climbing the ladder of education and well-being have failed to extend their hand to help their fellows on the rungs below. Civil rights leaders cannot with sit-ins change the fact that adults are illiterate. Marches do not create jobs for their children.   *November 3, 1965*

WHATEVER PEOPLE MAY feel about open housing or open schools—though I myself am deeply committed to both—still there can be no argument at all, no sense for even a committed segregationist, in the maintenance of Negro unemployment. Making sure men have jobs does not by itself mean that they will live with you, or that their children will go to school with you. It does not mean, in the long run, higher taxes or welfare costs; indeed, it means far less, and lessened costs of crime and crime prevention as well. It means the use of unused resources, and greater prosperity for all. Meeting the unemployment problem can only be to the benefit of every American of every shade of opinion ... People with jobs can buy or rent their own housing, people with adequate incomes can see that their children are educated; people with jobs can mark out their own relationships with their fellows of whatever color. But without employment, without basic economic security and self-sufficiency, any other help we provide will be only temporary in effect.

Remarks before Subcommittee on Executive Reorganization of the Committee on Government Operations of the United States Senate, December 10, 1966

BUT IF ANY man claims the Negro should be content or satisfied, let him say he would willingly change the color of his skin and go to live in the Negro section of a large city. Then, and only then, has he a right to such a claim.

Address, Berkeley Campus, University of California,
October 22, 1966

MANY MILLIONS OF white people, especially in the North—people who until recently assumed that the

Negro was satisfied with the great social progress of the past twenty years—are faced now with the startling discovery that it is not true, that whatever progress Negroes have made is inadequate to their need for equality.

August 27, 1964

IT IS AN honor and pleasure for me to accept the Stephen S. Wise Award for advancing human freedom. I am deeply grateful to you for choosing me to join so distinguished a list of recipients as President Truman, Prime Minister Ben Gurion and Senator Lehman.

Let me say that I am pleased, also, to accept this award because it typifies a different kind of brotherhood than that occasionally attributed to me—and my brothers.

Speech, American Jewish Congress, New York City,
October 28, 1962

IN RECENT MONTHS we have seen comment on what some have called the "blacklash." Opposition to violence and riots and irresponsible action is the justified feeling of most Americans, white and black. But that "backlash" which masks hostility to the swift and complete fulfillment of equal opportunity and treatment, which contains opposition to demands for justice and freedom, which denies the need to destroy slums, provide education and eliminate poverty—that is wrong, shameful, immoral and self-defeating. And any leader who seeks to exploit

this feeling for the momentary advantage of office
fails his duty to the people of this country.

Address, Berkeley Campus, University of California,
October 22, 1966

WE ARE USED to white faces; they blend into the
background; and too few people draw from Chicago's experience the lesson that lack of education—
and broken families—and crime—and poverty and
dependence—are color-blind.

Speech, National Council of Christians and Jews,
April 28, 1965

FOR THE AMERICAN Negro, the time has come.
Courts and Congresses and Presidents, in the name
of the country, have said that the color of a man's
skin shall no longer be a bar to the right to vote,
or learn, or work, or enter a public place. We have
held out the promise that color shall no longer stand
in the way of achievement or personal fulfillment or
keep a man from sharing in the affairs of the country. We have unveiled the prospect of full participation in American society, while television, radio
and newspapers bring to every Negro home the
knowledge of how rewarding such participation can
be. With so bountiful a promise how much greater
must be the frustration and the fury of the Negro—
especially the young Negro—who, desperately want-
ing to believe, and half-believing, finds himself con-
fined in slums, unable to get an education and a job,
confronted by the open prejudice and subtle hos-

tilities of a white world, and seemingly powerless to change his condition or shape his future. For him the progress of the past can count for little against the crushing awareness that his hopes for the future are beyond his reach for reasons which have little to do with justice or his worth as a man. Occasionally, broken hope and a deeply felt futility erupt in violence and extreme statements and doctrines. If we deny a man his place in the larger community then he may turn inward to find his manhood and identity, rejecting those he feels have rejected him. Therefore, far more impressive than the violence of a few is the fact that the overwhelming majority of American Negroes retain their faith in the good will of the nation and the possibilities of peaceful progress within the ordered framework of American politics and life.

Address, Berkeley Campus, University of California,
October 22, 1966

ON LAW, LAWYERS
AND COMMITTEES

PEOPLE KEEP BRINGING up the time when my brother
was looking for the best lawyer in the United States
to make Attorney General and happened to light on
me, and when he asked what was wrong with giving
me a little experience before I went out and prac-
ticed law. . . . You know, you can hear all that just
so long, and if you are a sensitive soul it begins to
affect you. . . . I would have thought it had gotten
through to . . . you that I got out of law school and
went to work in the Department of Justice as a
regular attorney in 1951. It is not as if I had had no
experience when I worked there. I worked very
hard. I took my work home at night. I was diligent,
industrious, and then ten years later I became
Attorney General.
Speech, Central High School, Philadelphia, Penn-
sylvania, May 6, 1964

IN GEORGE ORWELL's world of the future, the Min-

istry of Hate was called the Ministry of Love and
the Ministry of War was called the Ministry of
Peace. It must be the purpose of government to
insure that the Department over which I presided
is more than a Department of Prosecution and is, in
fact, the Department of Justice.   *July, 1964*

IN THE WORDS of the old saying, every society gets
the kind of criminal it deserves. What is equally
true is that every community gets the kind of law
enforcement it insists on.   *Speech, 1964*

WE ARE DEDICATED to the proposition that liberty
and law are inseparable; that we truly believe social
progress strengthens and enlarges freedom.
Address, Law Day Ceremonies, Virginia State Bar,
Roanoke, Virginia, May 1, 1962

CRIME IS NOT only a cause of economic waste, but
far worse than that, it is a reproach to the moral
pretensions of our society, and advertises to the
world the gap between our pronouncements and
our performance.
Address, American Bar Association House of Dele-
gates, San Francisco, California, August 6, 1962

LAWS AND SPEECHES do not build schools. They do
not put capable teachers in the schools. And they

do not give children the food, the clothing, the books and the encouragement they need if they are to stay in the shiny new school we build. Laws by themselves will not make a land reform—if farmers do not also have access to credit and technical assistance and fertilizers. Laws and economic aid and reforms by themselves will not create jobs—unless someone is determined to use these economic resources to create the jobs. Laws by themselves will not insure farm workers the minimum wage—unless we act to insure that the laws are enforced. And all our economic, social and material progress will be for nothing—if we do not at the same time move toward increasing freedom toward a society where all can freely speak and act to share in the decisions which shape their lives.

Remarks, Catholic University, Rio de Janeiro,
November 25, 1965

As LONG AS a man is handicapped before the bar of justice because of his poverty, our task as lawyers is not done.

Address, American Bar Association House of Delegates, San Francisco, California, August 6, 1962

THE MORE CLOSELY one looks at the cost and deployment of our crime prevention efforts, the more apparent it becomes that we have put too much responsibility at the end of the line, rather than at the beginning. Enforcement and correction can do only part of the job.　　　　　　*Speech, 1964*

WHENEVER MEN TAKE the law into their own hands, the loser is the law—and, when the law loses, freedom languishes.

Address before the Joint Defense Appeal of the American Jewish Committee and the Anti-Defamation League of B'nai B'rith, Chicago, Illinois, June 21, 1961

LEGAL SERVICES, particularly defense in criminal cases, are not like houses or automobiles where those with more money can buy better products without affecting the basic functioning of society. When one defendant cannot afford a complete defense, justice is being rationed.

Address, American Bar Association House of Delegates, San Francisco, California, August 6, 1962

IN OUR SOCIETY, laws are administered to protect and expand individual freedom, not to compel individuals to follow the logic other men impose on them.

Address, American Jewish Congress, New York City, October 28, 1962

IT IS MY conviction that there are few areas in our law which more urgently demand reform than our present unfair system of choosing the immigrants we will allow to enter the United States. It is a source of embarrassment to us around the world. It is a source of loss to the economic and creative strength of our nation as a whole.   *Speech, 1964*

THE LAW WHICH governs us must be written in the statute books. But there are areas in which our guide is more moral than legal—more a part of the basic fabric of humanity than a rigid code—more a part of our beliefs than specific rules of conduct.

Address, the 120th Anniversary Dinner of B'nai B'rith, Chicago, October 13, 1963

WHAT DO WE really mean, as lawyers, when we say that it is proper and constitutional to avail oneself of every legal defense? Surely the Canons of Ethics make clear the impropriety of using dilatory tactics to frustrate the cause of justice. We have only to imagine that principle being constantly applied across the board, in day-to-day litigation, to see that for all its validity it must be met by a counter principle, a concept that might be called the principle of good faith. Every lawyer knows that nothing but national chaos would result if all lawyers were to object to every interrogatory, resist every *subpoena duces tecum* and every disposition, seek every possible continuance and postponement, frame unresponsive pleadings and resist court orders to a point just short of contempt.   *September, 1964*

WE ARE A part of an intricate system that has developed over the centuries as man's best hope for resolving disputes and appraising policies—for working out solutions to problems. If this system of law— of equal justice for all—can be kept viable, and if people of all backgrounds and of all races and creeds can begin to fully understand and fully take advantage of it, then—and only then—will we stand to realize the promise of democracy, both for ourselves and for the world.

Address, Annual Meeting of the Missouri Bar Association, Kansas City, Missouri, September 27, 1963

THE ULTIMATE relationship between justice and law will be an eternal subject for speculation and analysis. But it may be said that in a democratic society law is the form which free men give to justice. The glory of justice and the majesty of law are created not just by the Constitution—nor by the courts—nor by the officers of the law—nor by the lawyers—but by the men and women who constitute our society—who are the protectors of the law as they are themselves protected by the law.

Address, Law Day Ceremonies of the Virginia State Bar, Roanoke, Virginia, May 1, 1962

LAWYERS HAVE THEIR duties as citizens but they also have special duties as lawyers. Their obligations go far deeper than earning a living as specialists in corporation or tax law. They have a continuing responsibility to uphold the fundamental principles of justice from which the law cannot depart.

Speech, Dedication of Kendrick Hall, University of San Francisco Law School, San Francisco, California, September 29, 1962

No GENERATION OF lawyers has yet failed its responsibility to the law or to our society. The role of the lawyer in de Tocqueville's time prompted him to say that "I cannot believe that a republic could hope to exist at the present time if the influence of lawyers in public business did not increase in proportion to the power of the people." Let us today continue to accept that challenge, whether in private practice or public service. Let us see to it that for all our citizens criminal law means criminal justice.   *October, 1964*

WE ARE FINDING that it is not enough to say that justice should be done—or even to pass laws commanding that justice be done.

THE RULE OF law in an open society still is a revolutionary ideal throughout much of the world. Our strength to transpose this ideal into reality throughout the world must depend over the years on our dedication to it at home.

Address, Portland City Club, Portland, Oregon,
October 6, 1961

I HAVE WAITED a long time for this visit to the Pacific Northwest. Mr. Justice Douglas has often assured me that it is the most beautiful and exciting part of the United States; and, as a mere Attorney General, who am I to argue against the Supreme Court?

Speech, Seattle World's Fair, August 7, 1962

SOME PEOPLE IN the world today do not see law
as the instrument of freedom and justice. Too frequently the whole tradition of *stare decisis* appears
to tie the law to the status quo; and a written constitution means little to a man who cannot remember
his last meal and does not know where his next one
is coming from.

Address, Law Day Ceremonies, Virginia State Bar,
Roanoke, Virginia, May 1, 1962

I AM ADVISEDLY aware that you have spent two long
days now celebrating your law school's golden anniversary. I suspect that the greatest virtue in any
more oratory will lie in its blessed brevity. If I had
any doubts on this score Father Callahan's letter of
invitation delicately enlightened me. He mentioned
that Father Connolly was recovering from a spinal
disc operation and also that the affair did not have to
last too long. I am not clear whether he was whisper-
ing a hint, a hope or a prayer. You can never be sure
with Father Callahan. But I'll try to keep in mind
that any old place in a speech is a wonderful place
to stop. I would not want any speech-induced dis-
comfort of Father Connolly to become a wide-spread
affliction of this assemblage.

Speech, University of San Francisco Law School,
San Francisco, California, September 29, 1962

WHAT IS THE price tag on equal justice under law?
Has simple justice a price which we as a profession

must exact? Is that what we have come to? It is certainly the way the underprivileged, the poor, the helpless regard us. Helplessness does not stem from the absence of theoretical rights. It can stem from an inability to assert real rights. The tenants of slums and public housing projects, the purchasers from disreputable finance companies, the minority group member who is discriminated against—all these may have legal rights which—if we are candid —remain in the limbo of the law.

Speech, University of Chicago Law School, Chicago, Illinois, May 1, 1964

THERE HAVE BEEN some comments about the Department of Justice awakening three newsmen in the middle of the night to ask some questions [during 1962 steel price crisis]. I want to tell you the reaction of your reporter, Louis Panos, who covers the Department of Justice for The Associated Press.

The next evening Mr. Panos came into my office and said: "I am just leaving for home and before I go to bed is there anything you'd really like to know?" Then he said, "Don't call me, I'll call you."

Associated Press Luncheon, New York City, April 23, 1962

IT IS POINTLESS to tell Negroes living in Northern slums to obey the law. To them, the law is the enemy . . . The only answer is massive relief with real help going to the young.   *July, 1967*

THE MOST ANY law can do is point the way—the
rest is up to the people. Civil rights is not an issue
that can be solved by governmental edict—it must
be dealt with at the community level, within states,
within cities, within neighborhoods—wherever a
meeting takes place between persons of light and
dark skin.

*Address, Annual Convention of the Theater Owners
of America, New York City, October 28, 1963*

THE THEORY OF the bail system—the only justification recognized for it by the courts—is that a bail
bond is necessary to insure the appearance of the
defendant at trial. In actual practice, the bail system
measures human freedom by financial ability.

*Speech, Academy of Trial Lawyers, Pittsburgh,
Pennsylvania, June 1, 1964*

I LOOK UPON the antitrust laws as being "pro-
business." I believe firmly that the purpose of the
antitrust laws is to protect and promote the competi-
tive interests of business, small and large, as well as
to protect the public.   *Speech, 1964*

IN A COMMITTEE HEARING *in 1957, the following exchange occurred between Robert Kennedy, a member of the McClellan Committee, and Dave Beck,
then head of the Teamsters Union:*
KENNEDY: Do you feel that if you gave a truthful

answer to this Committee on your taking of $320,000 of Union funds that might tend to incriminate you?

BECK: It might.

KENNEDY: Is that right?

BECK: It might.

KENNEDY: You feel that yourself?

BECK: It might.

KENNEDY: I feel the same way.

CHAIRMAN: We will have order, please.

KENNEDY: I want to know, breaking that money down, Mr. Beck, did you use Union funds to purchase five dozen diapers for some of your friends at $9.68?

Mr. Beck again invoked the Fourth and Fifth Amendments.

WIRETAPPING IS A subject of deepest concern to me. I do not believe in it. But I also believe we must recognize that there are two sides to the argument. In this regard it is interesting to note that when we introduced proposals revising the law on wiretapping I found that many critics had not even bothered to read the bill. I was further interested by the fact that the American Civil Liberties Union strenuously opposed the bill, while the ACLU's own president, former Attorney General Biddle, testified in favor of it.   *Speech, 1964*

IN AUGUST of 1957, Kennedy questioned James Hoffa during a committee hearing about a company which was owned by Mrs. Hoffa.

KENNEDY: Has this been a profitable operation?

HOFFA: You have the record. I think you could say that it was.

KENNEDY: Well, I am asking you the question.

HOFFA: Since it is not my company, I can only say that I think that it was.

KENNEDY: It was. You do not know? Your wife has not let you know how much money she made?

HOFFA: I think I know how much she made.

KENNEDY: Approximately, how much do you think she made in that company since it was set up?

HOFFA: I can't tell you, offhand, but a guess. I can give it to you this afternoon, if I can get it.

KENNEDY: We have some figures here.

HOFFA: Read them off, brother.

THE LAW OF the land imposes on all male citizens an obligation to perform military service. But barely half our young men serve as much as a day; only 40 percent of those now reaching the age of 26 have served for more than six months; and, as our younger age groups grow in size, a smaller proportion serve. Those who do serve are special also because they are more mentally and physically fit, more alert and capable than many of those who do not serve . . . But they are special for yet another reason: They serve because they have less money than others, equally well-qualified, who do not serve. By regulation, simply being in a college or university—for however many years, no matter the quality of the school or the importance of the course of study— guarantees a deferment. And as we all know, it is far more likely that as between two students of equal merit, the wealthier is far more likely to attend college. So our draft laws discriminate among our young men on the ground of wealth.

Statement, Senate Floor, July 16, 1965

DURING FIVE WEEKS *of investigation of coin-machine businesses in 1957, Kennedy had the following exchange with Milton Hammergren, vice president of the Wurlitzer Company, who freely admitted that he had gone to major underworld figures to handle distribution of juke boxes.*

KENNEDY: And the people that you found as a general rule—the only people that could get this distribution achieved—were these people with the underworld connections, as a practical matter?

Mr. Hammergren said that it was true and he described in detail the force, violence and terrorism that frequently accompanied distribution.

KENNEDY: Were company officials upset about the use of force?

HAMMERGREN: Company officials, of which I was one, yes, we didn't like it, but we still had to sell juke boxes. We all knew about it, and we knew what the problems were. We tried to go along with it the best we could.

KENNEDY: Even if it became necessary that somebody was killed during the course of it?

HAMMERGREN: Well, that is pretty broad, Mr. Kennedy. I don't think we would condone that knowingly, no.

KENNEDY: I mean if somebody, just in the course of trying to get your boxes distributed, if somebody was killed, that was taken as part of the trade?

HAMMERGREN: That is one of the liabilities of the business, I would say.

Now, AS ALWAYS, when the Constitution is too narrowly interpreted on a word-for-word basis, it can too easily become a crutch for reaction, a reactionalization, an excuse for maintaining the status quo. This is the very thing that Jefferson feared, so long ago, when he urged us not to regard the wording of the document with "sanctimonious reverence." My point is that the Constitution was never meant to specify every detail, every individual right in the relations of man to man in this country. It was intended to set forth certain duties of government and certain restrictions on government—nowhere in its wording does it pretend to tell us, as individual citizens, how to treat our neighbors. But what Woodrow Wilson called the *spirit* of the Constitution does, and has always done, just that. We must understand the spirit as well as the letter of the Constitution—the spirit that "will always be the spirit of the age."

Speech, Ceremonies Celebrating the 175th Anniversary of the Ratification of the Constitution, Independence Hall, Philadelphia, Pennsylvania, June 21, 1963

I THINK THOSE who refuse to abide by the decisions of our Supreme Court and of other courts weaken not only the authority of the courts, but our entire system of government. Basically, the only way that any decision of any court becomes effective, in a meaningful and stable way, is when compliance with it takes place voluntarily. Those who have resisted the implementation of Supreme Court decisions— like those who advocated massive resistance to the Brown decision in 1954—have undoubtedly caused the Court to suffer in the eyes of the nation. On the other hand, it is important not to stifle legitimate criticism of court decisions. The proper way to deal with criticism like that which followed the reapportionment decisions and the decisions protecting the constitutional rights of persons accused of crimes is to answer it through free and open discussion and debate. It would damage our society more, in my judgment, if we undertook to deal with such criticism by stifling it.

Television Interview, WTTG Studios, Metromedia
Television Network, May 15, 1966

ON YOUTH

THE YOUNG throughout the world will not wait for our concern. They are going ahead with their own revolution, not waiting for us. They are going ahead in their own way and in their own time. In many countries today they are in open revolt against oppression and against poverty, against the grinding condition of systems which have not allowed progress. They are in revolt against the established order, against the status quo. History is on their side, and in one way or another they will achieve a large measure of success in their endeavors, whatever the cost. In so many instances, their revolution is an easy decision for them, for they feel they have nothing to lose. What they think and what they do has a direct effect on all of us here in the United States. Across the globe they are a force of whirlwind proportions, and the world of tomorrow will bear the imprint of their ideals and their goals. For this reason, we must be concerned about them.

Delivered at the Commemoration of the 125th Year

of the Founding of Central High School, Philadel-
phia, Pennsylvania, May 6, 1964

EVERY GENERATION inherits a world it never made;
and, as it does so, it automatically becomes the
trustee of that world for those who come after. In due
course, each generation makes its own accounting
to its children.
Speech, Meeting of the University of South Carolina
Chapter, American Association of University Pro-
fessors, Columbia, South Carolina, April 25, 1963

IN SUCH A fantastic and dangerous world—we will
not find answers in old dogmas, by repeating out-
worn slogans, or fighting on ancient battlegrounds
against fading enemies long after the real struggle
has moved on. We ourselves must change to master
change. We must rethink all our old ideas and beliefs before they capture and destroy us. And for
those answers America must look to its young people, the children of this time of change. And we look
especially to that privileged minority of educated
men who are the students of America.
Speech, Worthington, Minnesota, September 17, 1966

OUR SOCIETY CHANGES rapidly; but we have not
provided enough opportunity for people to change
with it. We are proud, and justly, of the opportunities we offer to our young people; now as never
before, the lives of most of them are their own to

determine. But what we have tended to overlook is that most of our people have, between the ages of 15 and 20, been forced to make a choice—of life and education and career—and that one choice has sharply limited later opportunities. We know, from our experience under the GI bill, that millions of our young men have a potential for college work which is not brought out in the usual course of life. And that experience also teaches us that men in their late twenties, and thirties, and even older, can return to education and do as well or better than younger students. The price of today's missed opportunities is too high. The time has come when we must open the channels of opportunity—the chance for new labor and new lives—for all our citizens. *Address, Borough President's Conference of Community Leaders, January 21, 1966*

I FEEL WE can approach the young people of the world with strength and with confidence. We have made a representative government work, and maintained freedom at the same time. We have no apologies to make for what we have done here in the United States. We are big enough to admit our errors and strong enough to be tolerant of ideas and diversity. I think the advantage is irrepressible. No other system can match it in our conquest for inquiring young minds. We are a young nation, and we have in addition the strength, the spirit, the vigor to lead the world by our example. What we need is the discernment to identify true values and goals, however difficult that may be.

Speech, Commemoration of the 125th Year of the
Founding of Central High School, Philadelphia,
Pennsylvania, May 6, 1964

BUT FOR OUR young people, I suspect Vietnam is
a shock as it cannot be to us. They did not know
World War II, or even Korea. And this is a war
surrounded by rhetoric they do not understand or
accept; these are the children not of the Cold War,
but of the Thaw.

Address, Dinner—Americans for Democratic Action,
Philadelphia, Pennsylvania, February 24, 1967

I THINK THAT some of the demonstrations have
weakened the position of those who advocate a particular cause. But this doesn't mean they are illegal.
Unless they violate local or Federal laws, I don't
think that we have to take any legal action to protest ourselves. And I think the fact that so many
young people and so many other citizens are taking
such an active interest in this matter is healthy for
the country, whether they agree or disagree with
our present policy.

Television Interview in the WTTG Studios of the
Metromedia Television Network, May 15, 1966

WE KNOW THAT crime reaches its peak in the summer months, when young people are out of school
and too often out of work as well. A summer job—a
useful activity—an opportunity to earn money for

food, and clothing, and entertainment—can make the
difference between a boy who will go on to finish
school and contribute to the community—and a boy
who will be a constant threat and a burden to the
community all his life. When these boys are lost, we
are the losers. The Federal government has to act.
The State and the City have to act. But all their
activity and all these programs come down to one
question: will this boy, this real individual standing
in front of us, get a job?

Speech, Kings County Democratic Dinner, May 20,
1965

THE WONDROUS production machine which has
made us richer, as we count, than any people in
history, within which we all find sustenance and
support is a business economy—which is to say, that
most Americans are engaged in some form of business—indeed, that Coolidge was accurate, if not particularly edifying, when he said that "the business of
America is business." Yet we know that in a survey
last year, only 12 percent of all graduating college
seniors hoped for a career in business, or thought
such a career would be worthwhile and satisfying.
Why? Part of the answer, surely, is that the great
corporations which are so large a part of American
life, play so small a role in the solution of its vital
problems . . . Of course, it may well be argued that
the business of business is to make a profit, that to
attempt more is to do less than it stockholders deserve. But does such an argument have relevance,
ask the young, when a single company, like General

Motors or American Telephone and Telegraph, has annual profits greater than the gross national product of any one of seventy nations in the world?

Address, Dinner—Americans for Democratic Action,
Philadelphia, Pennsylvania, February 24, 1967

HERE IN AMERICA today, perhaps the clearest mirror of our performance, the truest measure of whether we live up to our ideals, is our youth.

Address, Dinner—Americans for Democratic Action,
Philadelphia, Pennsylvania, February 24, 1967

ALL OF US have the right to dissipate our energies and talent as we desire. But those who are serious about the future have the obligation to direct those energies and talents toward concrete objectives consistent with the ideals they profess. From those of you who take that course will come the fresh ideas and leadership, which are the compelling needs of America.

Address, Berkeley Campus, University of California,
October 22, 1966

ON EDUCATION

MANY OF YOU, I know, are approaching the end of your schooling. The time of graduation—and liberation—is upon you. This is a time when you must expect to endure a good many profound remarks about your past and your future, your obligations and your challenges. I hesitate to afflict you further—and am consoled only by the fact that I went through a comparable ordeal when I finished college a few years back and I can recall not one word of what was said. This gives me, I might add, a pleasant sense of irresponsibility today.

Address, California Institute of Technology, Pasa-
dena, California, June 8, 1964

I BELIEVE THE time has already come when the first two years of college—just like elementary school or high school—should be free to all qualified students.

Speech delivered at Sioux City, Des Moines, Marion
and Dubuque, Iowa, October 9, 1966

WE MUST REACH out as well to those who have been passed by in the past—those already out of school, the fathers and mothers of young children, the unemployed and the abandoned of this entire nation. Here we must recognize that education is not something—and cannot be allowed to be—something which, once interrupted, is over for life. We need new kinds of universities and colleges—able to teach, not only in fine buildings, but in community centers and parks and even in homes—colleges which are no more than groups of people determined that learning shall be brought to all those who need it.

Speech at Dedication of Mt. Providence Junior College, Baltimore, Maryland, September 12, 1966

REMEMBERING MY OWN graduation from college (which, people keep reminding me, wasn't really so very long ago), I think I can imagine something of what you feel this afternoon.

Speech delivered at Commencement Exercises, Trinity College, Washington, D.C., June 2, 1963

EDUCATION IS THE KEY to the future for every one of our children. In a world such as this, it does not matter what material goods we leave our children— but it is vitally important that we give them the best education that is available. There are those who think education a luxury and cooperation between Americans a socialist plot. They are for education, if the Federal government has no part in it; for education, but they must say what will be taught and what will not; for education, except if it costs money. But if this country is to keep its place of leadership in the world, if we are to be adequate to the unprecedented challenges we face, then we must have education—not education but, not education if, not education except; we need the most of the best education it is within our power to give to our children. And we must acknowledge, at another level, that all our educational systems have not successfully educated millions of poor children—not just in Watts and Harlem, but in Appalachia and on Indian reservations and among the mentally retarded as well.

Statement at Dinner Honoring Congressman James C. Corman, Sportsmen's Lodge, Los Angeles, California, October 21, 1966

THE PRESIDENT'S PANEL on Mental Retardation estimated that there are 75,000 mentally retarded children of servicemen who present special problems and require special facilities. This number includes those who can be helped with special education classes and occasional training by therapists. But it also includes the profoundly and severely retarded— those children who are non-educable and often non-trainable. Frequently, physical deformities and handicaps accompany these cases of severe retardation . . . As a nation we try to insure that each individual receives the full measure of medical and psychological care and therapeutic assistance that is available today. However, in the area of service dependents, we have failed to meet and cope with the problems of retardation, mental illness and physical handicaps . . . It is inconceivable in a society which strives to aid the mentally retarded, and in a time when the utmost is demanded of our men in uniform, that these families can be left to their own devices in seeking a solution to such heart-rending problems.   *Statement, U. S. Senate, April 1, 1966*

IN THIS MOBILE society, with most Americans moving across state lines at least once in their lifetime, the education of a child in Iowa contributes to the whole nation—and a stunted education elsewhere can force Iowa to spend more on welfare and police and housing. Education is a national resource; it should be paid for on a national basis, with each paying his share as a citizen of the nation.
Speech delivered at Des Moines, Iowa, October 9,
1966

WHY SHOULD WE not raise money locally each year to send some of our brightest boys and girls to schools overseas—and receive in exchange children from foreign countries in our schools? And I would add that I would not necessarily limit the exchange to countries on our side of the iron curtain. This program should not have to be done just by the Federal Government or under its direction.
Address, Joint Defense Appeal of the American
Jewish Committee and the Anti-Defamation League
of B'nai B'rith, Chicago, Illinois, June 21, 1961

THESE BASIC DECISIONS [to subsidize private groups] were not made unilaterally by the CIA, but by officials in the executive branch in the Eisenhower, Kennedy, and Johnson administrations . . . I think it is unfair that the CIA should take the blame for this. Any of these decisions made by the CIA had to have been approved by others.

Press Conference, Senate Office, Washington, 1967

WHENEVER I RECEIVE an award or am present when other people receive an award it takes me back to my days in high school and in college. . . . You know, when the graduating class gave the award for the best athlete and for the best scholarship and for the person who was best in Latin, and best in Greek, and who wrote the best composition—I received a prize for being the fellow with the fifth best sense of humor in my graduating class.

Delivered before the Philadelphia Fellowship Commission, April 3, 1962

WE WILL, in a sense, have to make of the United States a vast continuing educational system—so that our education will not end at a particular age, a particular point in time, but will continue through life . . . If we would continue as the most favored and fortunate of nations, we must be the most prepared and educated of nations. This will require great new efforts in education. For all of our people deserve the chance to catch up to progress.

Speech prepared for delivery at University of Vermont, Burlington, Vermont, September 24, 1966

FAR TOO OFTEN in our society, the school, the college or the university seem, to the poor, remote and inaccessible. With its formal structure, its "downtown" language and phrases, . . . it seems forbidding, powerful and alien. Too often, it is. To change this, we must reapproach the whole question of cooperation among educational institutions. Here, we are not discussing an arrangement for sharing of faculties, or even of students, but rather of fundamental rearrangements. For example, we have discovered in the elementary grades, that the "ungraded" school or class has great advantages. A child who can perform with his peers or beyond in one field, may lag behind in another. Even many labeled as mentally retarded have some times performed near-genius work in particular areas. Operation Headstart has taught us that remedial work can begin before there is anything to remedy. Why not, then, apply this learning to the entire process? Why not view all of the schools as one school, one education?

Speech at Dedication of Mt. Providence Junior College, Baltimore, Maryland, September 12, 1966